THIS BOOK BELONGS TO

_____

an ultimate hunter

The

ULTIMATE HUNTER'S HANDBOOK

DAVID & KARIN HOLDER
with LARRY DUGGER

HARVEST HOUSE PUBLISHERS
EUGENE, OREGON

The Ultimate Hunter's Handbook
Copyright © 2020 by David Holder, Karin Holder, and Larry Dugger
Published by Harvest House Publishers
Eugene, Oregon 97408
www.harvesthousepublishers.com

ISBN 978-0-7369-7781-4 (pbk.)
ISBN 978-0-7369-7782-1 (eBook)

Library of Congress Cataloging-in-Publication Data is on file at the Library of Congress, Washington, DC.

Printed in the United States of America

20 21 22 23 24 25 26 27 28 / VP-SK / 10 9 8 7 6 5 4 3 2 1

Take your bow and a quiver full of arrows,
and go out to the open country
to hunt some wild game for me.
GENESIS 27:3 NLT

CONTENTS

INTRODUCTION

The *Ultimate Hunter's Handbook*...that's a pretty bold statement, wouldn't you say? But once you understand the amount of time, effort, and information contained in the pages you're about to read, then you'll know where we're coming from. This book is the documentation of our family's journey in the outdoors. It's filled with the mistakes and lessons that ultimately led to our success. In our opinion, failure can be a good teacher if you're willing to learn from it.

The stories you are about to read have been resurrected in order to bring laughter, learning, and helpful information to your next hunt and your everyday life. As you read, keep in mind that our family's definition of success isn't shooting the next record-book buck or a bull elk large enough to create a name for yourself. To the Holders, success is that you were there, fully present in the hunt, and that you're fulfilled because you gave your best effort. You placed yourself in a moment of time where everything else seemed to fade away in the excitement of the chase.

We are happy to provide you with the details and strategies we've learned while stalking our wild adversaries. Sometimes we win (while hunting), and sometimes we learn. But each encounter we have with a wild animal is meaningful and memorable. We treat each hunt with respect and reverence, knowing that hunting has taught us more about life and ourselves than we ever could have learned in a classroom or lecture hall. The very existence of the wild game we pursue drives us to go places we never thought we could. Their uncanny ability to know our next move fuels us to look at who we are and reflect on the reasons why we do what we do.

When we immerse ourselves in God's outdoor classroom, we see, hear, smell, and feel things that most people don't even know exist. Some days, it's the beauty of a sunrise. On other days, it's hearing the high-pitched roar of a bull elk bugling in the canyon just a few yards from where we are standing. No matter the scenario, all of us here at *Raised Hunting* have been transformed in some way by the time we spend enjoying the outdoors.

The Ultimate Hunter's Handbook documents not only some of our successes but also plenty of trial and error—both in the woods and on our journey of faith. It's filled with ideas about how you can find your way through your next wild-animal encounter as well as your next spiritual encounter. After all, the ultimate hunter is Jesus because He is hunting for all of us…and I've heard His aim is true!

WHAT TO EXPECT

Each chapter is broken down into four easy-to-read sections, all designed to help you become an ultimate hunter. Read each section carefully and use the insights gleaned from my family's outdoor successes and failures to help you be your best—spiritually, physically, mentally, and on the hunt. These are the four sections:

David's Pro Tip

Over the years, I've accumulated a vast knowledge of both the animals we hunt and the conditions necessary to safely and effectively harvest them. In this portion, I will share with you some of my best tips and tactics (most of which I've learned the hard way).

David's Life Tip

Life is a lot like hunting. The things that make us good hunters are often the same things that make us successful in our everyday routines.

The lessons I've learned while enjoying the outdoors have guided me in marriage, parenting, friendship, and even my faith in God. Here, you will see how being an ultimate hunter goes hand in hand with being an ultimate human being.

David's Faith Tip

Karin and I are Christians, and our faith guides us, but it hasn't always been that way. Here, I will be transparent about my relationship with God and how it's taken me a while to figure out how to walk with Him. If you're interested in strengthening your walk with God and overcoming anything negative from your past, then you'll love this portion.

Encouragement from Karin

I (Karin) have been a follower of Christ for most of my life. I've learned to lean on Him for answers, direction, and sometimes sanity! I have written a few short devotions for this book that I believe will enhance your walk with God and give you some additional insight into how much the outdoor lifestyle really means to me. Use these mini faith tips to strengthen your relationship with the One who gave us the outdoors to enjoy.

Harvest Log

How many times have you enjoyed a hunt only to forget the key details of why it was so amazing? Over the course of my (David's) 40-year hunting career, I've kept detailed logbooks. Doing so allows me to revisit any hunt that I've been on in the past. At the end of this book, you'll find some of my blank harvest logs for you to use as you remember everything from the animal to the shot! Keeping a harvest log is also a great way to pass on your love of hunting to your children or grandchildren.

Godspeed and good hunting!
David

THE POST

David Holder

It's simple when we think about our lives like the fence lines that we pass every day. Some fence lines are straight and true, while others are crooked and loose. Eventually, they will all be broken and worn. But the ones that are built correctly and well cared for will stand the test of time.

If the fence lines represent life, then a fence post would represent a father and the connectors a mother. The post is what holds the fence up, while the connectors hold it all together. Our kids are the wire, jagged and barbed, running for miles, always reliant on the post and the connectors to keep them in place. If all the pieces stay connected, the fence will remain strong. The connector tightly holds the post to the wire, but the piece that determines whether the fence stands or falls will always be the post.

1

HOW YOU DO ANYTHING IS HOW YOU DO EVERYTHING

How You Practice Is How You Hunt

While hunting, I've made just about every mistake known to man. I have a list of blunders a mile long. I've misjudged creeks that I was sure would only be ankle deep at best, only to find out that unless my ankles were growing out of my armpits, the creek was a lot deeper than I thought! I've hiked the most rugged terrain in pursuit of the big one, only to find that poor optics had me stalking a deer that wasn't even legal in the unit I was hunting. I've set decoys in the wrong spots and facing the wrong way. I have rattled for deer when I should have been quiet, and I've silently hunted turkeys when I should have been calling.

Some of our mistakes stand out more than others, and some can even alter everything we do in the future as hunters. I remember one particular occasion when I made a mistake I had often warned against. I wasn't living by my own advice; I wasn't practicing what I had been preaching to others.

On this hunt, I hadn't been in the tree stand for more than five minutes when a buck showed up. It was as if he had followed me to my stand. In the predawn blackness, all I could do was stand there and listen to what sounded like a big-bodied buck chasing a doe in circles around the base of the tree I had just climbed. Time and time again, I strained my eyes in hopes of catching a flash of horns, but I couldn't see anything. To make matters worse, I was unfamiliar with my surroundings. I was in a new deer stand in a state where I had never hunted. I was there because I knew Illinois offered better whitetail hunting than I was used to in Montana. And by the sound of the ruckus below me, I had arrived smack-dab in the middle of the rut.

It was too early to see, much less shoot. But as streaks of red and orange began to peek over the horizon, glimpses of the deer surrounding me slowly came into view. There was more than one buck! And they began to grunt and fight. I could hear leaves rustling in front of me and behind me as if several deer were coming and going. There were now at least two and possibly three bucks directly under my stand.

Over the years, I've always considered myself an organized and ready hunter. I have stressed to my boys, Warren and Easton, that they should never go into the woods without being fully prepared. On this hunt, I would have to eat those words…

Release attached to my wrist, check. Quiver full of arrows, check. Grunt call in my right pocket, check. Range finder right beside me, check. I had thought of everything. So what could possibly go wrong? Well…in the past, every time I'd get into a deer stand or ground blind, one of the first things I'd do was bring my bow to full draw. Moving it to the left and then to the right, making sure I had range of motion and all was clear. But on that morning, in all the commotion, I hadn't taken the time to do that.

Now in the still-shadowy breaking dawn, I could just make out the largest buck's main beams as he walked straight toward me. It was time for me to grab my bow from the hanger and do what I had come all the way to Illinois to do—arrow a Midwest monster. Even in the low light, I could tell the buck was huge and far bigger than anything I had ever harvested. He was now standing broadside at eight yards and looking back at a smaller buck that had come to try to steal his doe. This was my opportunity to reach full draw without being detected. With my bow in my left hand, I maneuvered my right hand to try to hook my release onto the string. I didn't even need to look down—I had practiced for this moment so often that I could have done it hanging upside down with my eyes closed. But something was wrong—the trigger on my release was jammed. The jaws wouldn't open, so I couldn't clip it on the string. I tried and tried again, but nothing. If you've ever had a mature whitetail at close range, you know what it's like to have your heart beating out of your chest. My pounding heart sank as I realized the moment was about to slip through my fingertips—and all because I wasn't prepared.

Panicked and shaken, I didn't know what to do. I had another release in my pack but didn't have much hope I could remove the broken release, reach into the fanny pack for the replacement, and strap it on my bow before the deer got spooked and took off. But at this point, I had nothing to lose. With quiet, careful movements, I hung up my bow, slowly unzipped my pack, and took out my spare. So far so good. Or was it? For the second time that morning, I was faced with my own failure to practice what I preached.

I had taught hunting seminars during the months leading up to this hunt, and I had stated emphatically that something as noisy as Velcro has no business anywhere in a hunter's gear bag. I had already replaced the Velcro strap on the release I was using that day with a buckle. But I hadn't replaced the Velcro on my spare release. So there I was with a true giant standing at eight yards, a release that wouldn't work, and a replacement release that needed to be un-Velcroed and slipped on my wrist before the buck decided to walk away.

As I was working the Velcro loose, the buck looked up for the first time, causing me to slow my work even more. Frantic, I could see his posture changing, and he started to walk back up the trail he had just come down. Continuing to work on my release and trying to be as quiet as possible, I surrendered to the fact that he was out of bow range and I still didn't have the release open enough to slide over my wrist. I watched the monster buck walk out of sight.

Feeling the weight of failure and frustration, I slumped my

shoulders. I turned around and sat down. Trying to keep tears at bay, I looked down at the two releases. Why had I not taken my own advice and removed the Velcro on that second release? If only I had practiced what I had preached, I would have been sitting next to one of those Midwest monsters, proudly posing for a picture. Instead, I was sitting in a tree, disappointed in the events of the morning. At that moment, I was anything but an ultimate hunter.

Sulking and fiddling with the release that had failed, I learned my second lesson. Never crawl through a briar patch with your release buckled to your hand without checking to see if a thorn could be keeping it from opening. That is exactly what I had done that morning while trying to find my hunting spot where all this went down.

So know where you're going before you go, especially when it comes to a new hunting area. No matter what, check your equipment immediately upon arrival, and never have Velcro in your gear bag. And finally, ultimate hunters never preach to others what they won't do themselves. Remember, how you practice is how you hunt. I finished that morning without seeing one more deer, but I now realize that I didn't really fail because I learned something. And the next time I saw that deer, he wasn't so lucky…but that's another story.

DAVID'S LIFE TIP

How You Practice Is How You Play

Practicing to hunt is one thing; practicing or readying yourself for a successful life is another. In my past (before Raised Hunting), I was a firefighter. I'm still proud of all those years, and as I look back on my career, I like to think I was pretty good at my job. Don't get me wrong—I still made mistakes, and for a guy like me, mistakes of any kind are hard to swallow. Some might call me a type-A personality. Others might describe me as being a bit obsessive-compulsive. Any way you cut it, I allow as little room as possible for error or failure, especially when it comes to something that can be avoided with a little effort and planning.

During my training with the fire department, I found a flaw that sticks with me to this day. A flaw that could have ended tragically, but by the grace of God, it didn't. What I experienced was so profound that it currently finds its way into my coaching, seminars, speaking engagements, and our Raised at Full Draw hunting camps. I can sum it up for you in one sentence: You must practice exactly how you expect to play because you will play exactly how you practice.

That statement never meant so much to me as it did the night my crew and I responded to an automobile accident involving two cars. Upon arrival, I saw a woman crying uncontrollably in one of the vehicles. She had rear-ended a large flatbed truck, and her small sports car was jammed into a spot where it was never meant to fit. Her seat belt was the only thing that had kept her from lunging forward into the dash that was now collapsed on her legs. She was lucky to be alive. Comforting her wasn't easy, but I reassured her that we were going to do everything in our power to get her out safely and that she needed to trust us and do what we told her to do.

The thick coating of blood on the driver's door told me that her left arm was badly cut, but I couldn't see the rest of her body or see how she was pinned. I explained to her, in detail, what we were going to do to get her free, and I added that she and I would have to work together. My demeanor calmed her, and for the first time, she was able to utter a few words between the sobs. "I'm pregnant," she said.

A pregnant victim is even more of a challenge, and before I could let anyone on my crew know what she had just revealed, I saw one of them approaching the car. In his left hand, he had a hydraulic tool we use for forcing doors and other pieces of metal out of the way, allowing us access to the patient. In his right hand, I could see what we referred to as a "punch." A punch is a spring-loaded metal pin that shatters glass without causing the glass to explode like it would if you hit it with a hammer. However, it still had the potential, especially when under pressure, to break the glass into hundreds of sharp pieces. Our protocol was to cover the patient before breaking the glass. We had practiced this maneuver hundreds of times before.

Protocol—during training exercises—was to break the glass on the windows and then push it into the car instead of pulling it out. We did this during training so we wouldn't leave an excessive amount of glass in our training locations. The same protocol stated that while working an actual accident, we would verbalize that we had covered the patient and would pull the glass out to avoid cutting the person we were extracting.

That all sounded great, but after several repetitions over weeks and months of training, I couldn't get the words out fast enough that night to stop my crew from breaking the driver side glass and pushing it in on the young mother. She screamed as the glass broke, and then she wailed, "My baby, my baby!"

I wanted to be mad at my crew for making such a simple yet possibly tragic mistake, but I couldn't be. They had done exactly what they had practiced so many times. I felt horrible and feared the worst, thinking we had done more damage to the young mother or possibly even harmed her unborn baby. Even though we successfully extracted her and delivered her to the emergency room with no life-threatening injuries, I could not shake the feeling of failure. She even wrote a letter of appreciation to the fire department for how my crew conducted themselves that night. However, nothing she or anyone else can say will ever erase the powerful lesson that was permanently imprinted upon my brain. Practice exactly how you expect to play because you will play exactly how you practice.

When I wake up every morning, I'm preparing myself for the real thing. I'm not just a good husband, father, friend, and follower of Christ in theory until a real emergency requires me to be all those things for real. I practice being those things from the moment my feet hit the floor. And my hope is that you will too.

SHOOT 'EM IN THE SHINY SPOT

If a turkey can't stand up, it can't fly away.

As bowhunters, we all know that feeling of pride and accomplishment that comes with harvesting an animal ethically. Whether I'm holding the bow or operating the camera for someone in my family, a clean kill is always a top priority. I believe if an animal is going to give its life, then I should do my best to take that life with as much dignity and respect as possible.

No matter where you live, you probably have a huntable population of wild turkeys within driving distance of your house. Bowhunting for turkeys is a great way to sharpen your shooting skills, and it gives you something else to chase right before deer season comes back around. Hunting wild turkeys with a bow is addicting and exciting. As I tell those who attend my seminars, turkey hunting is just like elk hunting. The only difference is, when your arrow strikes gold on a turkey, you can pick him up, throw him over your shoulder, and walk out. If you can do that with an elk, let me know. I want to elk hunt with you!

Getting the arrow in the right spot in order to make a quick kill is always an issue while turkey hunting. The wild turkey seems to be the animal most often lost by bowhunters, even after shooting a fatal shot. Shooting turkeys is tricky because they can fly. Also, because of the way their feathers are configured and their small stature, they don't bleed well. In fact, they might not leave a blood trail at all. Because of their unique ability to leave the scene quickly without a trace of blood, many turkeys are fatally shot but never found.

Fortunately for me, I got lucky one day after I had made a bad shot on a turkey. Actually, that bad shot turned out to be the best thing that has ever happened to me in all my years of turkey hunting. A big tom was strutting in front of me at 12 yards, and the pin on my bow sight was almost centered on him—slightly forward to guarantee a heart shot. But when I released the arrow, for whatever reason, the shot was about four inches low and four inches to the left. This caused my arrow to enter directly into his drumstick. Immediately, I thought, *Oh no! What have I done?* But my concern quickly disintegrated as I watched the big bird flopping on the ground. At first, I thought

I had just gotten lucky, but as I investigated my shot placement a few hours later, I realized my arrow had done its job. First, it broke both legs. Second, it didn't go all the way through. Third, it had punched a hole in both wings, rendering the bird helpless to leave. In addition to the skeletal damage, the arrow had also pierced the bottom portion of the torso, slicing through some of the vital organs.

I had accidentally found what I now refer to as the "shiny spot." Here, a carefully placed arrow will guarantee the recovery of your tasty trophy. For the best results, I recommend a rear expandable broadhead. I realize that there are other effective arrow placements as well, but I believe if you shoot a turkey in the shiny spot, you are more likely to find them. If a turkey can't stand up, it can't fly. A turkey is so heavy, it needs the space under its wings for takeoff. If both legs are broken and both wings are punctured, you will find him because he will be right where you shot him.

DAVID'S FAITH TIP

Practice What You Preach

When you look back at the two stories I shared in this chapter, you can clearly see that in your everyday life and in your hunting career, you have to practice if you want to be productive in the real thing. I believe if you aren't going to practice correctly, you shouldn't play at all.

For years, I never considered going to church to be a big deal. I mistakenly felt as though I was closer to God when I was hunting than I could ever be in a building—including a building made for worship. Don't misunderstand—I still love connecting with God through time spent in the outdoors, but it's actually because of the church that I love the outdoors even more.

A few years ago, our youngest son, Easton, suggested that Karin and I come with him to a church that he was interested in checking out. Reluctantly, I agreed to attend, knowing that I really didn't need to be there—or so I thought. When we walked in that morning, I was sure that this would be my first and last time through those doors. But soon after we sat down and I began to listen to the pastor, I started feeling something that I had never felt in a tree stand. I can't explain it other than to say…it felt right. Peace and comfort washed over me as I paid attention and soaked it all in.

Here we are a few years later, and while I wish I could tell you I make it to church every week, I can't honestly say that I do. But what I can say is that now I make every attempt to be there rather than making every attempt to be somewhere else. I now realize that the feeling I get sitting in a tree stand talking to God is enhanced by the time I spend sitting in church, building a relationship with Him. Finding the right church has reconditioned me and heightened my awareness and my attention to the details that really matter.

Somehow, going to church and showing God that I want to be faithful, both in my thoughts and in my actions, makes hunting mean even more.

Most of the time, you will find me either hunting or practicing hunting. But on most Sunday mornings, you will find me in the house of the Lord giving thanks. It's taken me a while, but I'm thankful that I can now say when it comes to God and me, I practice what I preach. And since I'm being completely honest—I may go to church on Saturday night if the weather forecast looks perfect for hunting on Sunday morning!

> So, friends, we can now—without hesitation—walk right up to God, into "the Holy Place." Jesus has cleared the way by the blood of his sacrifice, acting as our priest before God. The "curtain" into God's presence is his body.
>
> So let's *do* it—full of belief, confident that we're presentable inside and out. Let's keep a firm grip on the promises that keep us going. He always keeps his word. Let's see how inventive we can be in encouraging love and helping out, not avoiding worshiping together as some do but spurring each other on, especially as we see the big Day approaching (Hebrews 10:19-25 MSG).

———— ENCOURAGEMENT FROM KARIN ————

Don't Worry—Pray

"I can do all things through him who strengthens me" (Philippians 4:13 ESV).

Sometimes life feels like a walk in the park—Jurassic Park!

I'm slowly learning that life seldom goes as planned. What I thought would come easy, usually comes with challenges. I remember one particular hunt when all the cards were stacked against David and me. Although we had a strategy for approaching a specific tree stand that morning, for some reason, David changed his mind concerning the route we would take to get there. That wasn't uncommon, and I've learned over the years not to question David's God-given instincts, so I silently followed along.

As our short walk stretched into a very long walk, I started to get a bit worried. It was mid-November and unseasonably cold. While getting dressed that morning, well before the sun came up, I'd made sure to layer properly. I was prepared for a few hours of sitting still, and the last thing I wanted was to be cold while waiting for a shooter buck to come into range. Now walking farther and faster than I had originally anticipated, I could feel the sweat starting to drip down my spine. To make matters worse, I was carrying my bow and a heavy backpack. *Wonderful*, I thought. *I'm going to be soaked with sweat by the time we get there.*

The sun was starting to peek over the horizon, and David began to pick up the pace. No question now, I was dripping wet…and so was he.

Once we finally arrived, we climbed into the tree and began the process of getting ready to hunt. This is an important step you cannot skip—even if you are hot, sweaty, and a bit irritated that your husband chose to take the long way. I hung up my rattling horns and ranged three different distances with my range finder. I had to be sure I would know how far the deer might be, should one show up. I placed an arrow on my rest, and then David and I did an opening interview for our show *Raised Hunting*.

I noticed the wind had unexpectedly shifted and was now blowing our scent in the direction we were anticipating the deer to come from. Not good. Frustrated, I began to think of all the mistakes we had made that morning. We were late getting in the stand and covered in sweat, and now the wind had changed directions. With the cold temperatures, I was sure I would not be able to last an hour before freezing out. I knew getting sweaty before sitting on a cold day was a big mistake. Hypothermia can set in quickly. I was worried our morning sit was going to be cut short, and I knew if that were the case, we had no one to blame but ourselves.

I prayed at that moment, *God, I'm cold, and we have messed up this morning, but I trust You and know that things will work out.* That prayer calmed me a bit, and the feeling of worry began to slip away. You may think it strange that I pray about hunting, but the truth is, I pray about everything.

I decided to take my coat off to "air out" a bit. Keeping dry would be the key to staying warm. The wind shifted back to the direction we had originally anticipated, and it wasn't long until a doe walked by... then a little buck, and then a little bigger buck. Things were getting busy, and if I was going to get my coat back on, I knew I had to do it before anything big enough to shoot showed up. Just as I zipped my coat, David whispered, "There's a buck...a good one." The doe that had walked by our stand not more than an hour ago was leading him straight toward us. He walked to the edge of the timber and suddenly made a sharp left turn. If he continued, he would pass by at 17 yards completely broadside.

Ice crystals shimmered like diamonds woven through the buck's thick winter coat as the sun shone down. His breath clouded the air as he searched for his doe with every exhale. It was one of the most beautiful scenes a hunter could ask for. As he passed a small tree, I took the opportunity to pull back my bow, and when he emerged on the other side, I stopped him and released the arrow. My arrow found its mark, and the buck only ran about 50 yards before toppling over.

Just an hour before, I was praying that I would be able to stay in the stand that morning without freezing out, and now I wasn't even cold. God had answered my prayer and picked up the worry I'd laid at His feet.

God is always there, steady, ready, and waiting for us to share our thoughts with Him. If you're doubting or worried, reach out and let the One who causes the sun to rise help you rise.

REFLECTION

What's got you worried? How will you lay that down at the feet of your heavenly Father?

Cast all your anxiety on him because he cares for you.
1 PETER 5:7

2

DON'T SHOOT

Avoid Risky Shots

I've learned over the years that it's far better to not take a poor shot than risk making a bad shot. I would rather miss an opportunity to harvest an animal than take a chance on possibly wounding it.

I think the real question is, Why take those risky shots in the first place? Could it be that in your mind, the moment you've been dreaming of is finally here and you can't let it pass? That all the hard work, persistence, and sacrifice are about to pay off in one glorious moment as you watch your prey fall to the ground? What you do when the shot angle isn't right, the distance is too far, or something is blocking your view of an animal's vitals indicates whether you are an ultimate hunter. Will you take the shot and hope for the best, or will you do what's in the best interest of the animal by not risking injury? How will you win that all-too-familiar argument with yourself when the buck of a lifetime isn't presenting you with the opportunity to make a quick and humane kill?

Passing up the chance to harvest any animal is almost impossible—especially when you believe you will never get that opportunity again. You can even convince yourself that it's now or never. After all, you don't want to just hunt; you want to bring home the fruits of your labor. I know I've felt the pressure to fill a tag when I should have just been happy to be doing what I love—spending time outdoors with my friends and family.

One day, my buddy and I were hunting in the Judith Mountains of Montana, and we were having a horrible time getting just one of the 20 or 30 bulls in a large herd of elk to come our way. The thing that still stands out most is the sheer number of elk that were packed into the small meadow. What we experienced that morning was like something right out of *National Geographic*. There were big bulls herding dozens of cows, while smaller satellite bulls circled like sharks as they tried to lure one cow away from the rest.

Still, as we sat there in awe of what we were witnessing, I felt that we had come to do more than just watch. We had come to try to get an arrow into one of those lovesick bulls. I thought that it would be easy and that with so many to choose from, all I would have to do is call, wait, and let an arrow fly. But as usual, this hunt didn't go as I had expected.

As the sun began to rise, the huge herd had diminished to only a few animals. Most of the elk had already started to exit the meadow and were heading back into the canyon across from us. Not a single bull paid any attention to my best calling. No matter what I did to try to convince them to come our way, nothing was working. The problem we faced was simply getting close enough. Plus, we didn't have permission to hunt where the elk were currently located. Each day, the plan was the same. We needed to lure a bull away from the big herd.

On our last day, in desperation, we decided to try something new. I suggested that we slip around to the southern side of the herd, which would keep the wind in our favor. I felt that somehow getting closer to the animals might be a way to get a bull's attention. My hunting partner agreed. It really was now or never on this hunt.

We hadn't made it very far when a nearby bugling bull stopped us in our tracks. I hit a cow call, and once again, the bull screamed back. He was right in front of us! Our original plan was to split up so one of us could call the bull past the shooter. But before we could take more than two steps, three bulls appeared at less than 30 yards. As one of the bulls passed by a large cedar bush, I came to full draw. We had gone from nothing responding to our calls to having three bulls practically right on top of us. I stood in the open with my bow fully drawn. The bulls were now quartering toward us at less than 10 yards. They were looking hard and trying to figure out why I wasn't the cow elk they were expecting. I remained motionless, contemplating what I should do next. The bull I wanted to shoot was standing in such a way that his thick shoulder blocked his vitals. Even at 15 yards, I knew I didn't have a high percentage shot. At that moment, I did what a lot of hunters do: I tried talking myself into a shot that I knew was impossible. I told myself, *All you have to do is hit one lung. He won't be able to survive that. Besides, if you don't shoot, you won't get another chance.* Even though I knew trying to harvest this elk was a terrible idea, I had convinced myself that I could do it.

I touched the trigger on my release and watched the arrow travel less than 10 yards. I hit the elk exactly where I was aiming. My initial thought was pure joy as the arrow penetrated his right shoulder and was buried all the way to the fletching. But my excitement quickly disappeared as we watched the three elk run up the ridge directly across from us. I sat down and lifted my binoculars. The elk were at least half a mile away when they stopped to look back for the first time. I could see the fletching sticking out of the wounded bull, the arrow hadn't passed through, and I had only injured an otherwise healthy animal. I can still taste the bitterness of my stupid decision that day.

The last time I saw that elk was about one minute later as he topped the ridge and descended into the valley out of sight. The bull wasn't the only one who felt stabbed in the gut. I felt it as well. The elk didn't deserve that kind of treatment, and I almost quit bowhunting after that. I remember saying to myself, *David Holder, if you can't control your actions any better than that, then you don't deserve to be in the woods with a weapon in your hand.*

Don't get me wrong, I know that killing is a part of hunting. But I also believe that if you don't take the life of any animal as quickly as possible, you are a killer and not a hunter. A big part of being an ultimate hunter is knowing when to let down your bow (or gun) and realizing that by letting down your weapon, you aren't letting yourself down—you're actually holding up the very animals you pursue.

DAVID'S LIFE TIP

Not Every Opportunity Is a Good One

Anyone who knows me will tell you how seriously I take the harvesting of the animals we hunt. In my opinion, knowing when not to shoot is more important than knowing when to shoot. And even though the goal of every hunter is to take the life of an animal, I believe that life should be taken as humanely, respectfully, and ethically as possible. Part of your responsibility as an ultimate hunter is to honor the animals you hunt by learning how to safely and effectively harvest them.

Occasionally, while hunting, you will be faced with a dilemma. Will you do what is in the best interest of the animal, or will you do what you believe is in your best interest? Believe it or not, this also translates into your regular everyday life. You will make all kinds of decisions during your lifetime. Some will be good, and others won't. If you go back and look at the decisions that turned out to be less than the best, there is a good chance that in that moment of indecision, your gut was telling you not to do it. Some people call that instinct, while others might say it is intuition. I think it's God's way of helping you stay on track. I've been on this earth for more than 50 years, and I wish I had learned early in my life to "let down" and not force my way forward. I would be a lot further down the road in every aspect—not just hunting.

If you've been around me for any length of time, you have probably heard me talking about Raised at Full Draw—our archery camp for young kids and women. What you might not know is how these hunting camps came about. In 2002, a volunteer from the Rocky Mountain Elk Foundation called and asked me to teach elk calling at a camp for young hunters, and I happily agreed. I had no idea how a weekend with a handful of kids would have a profound influence on my future. After the camp was over, I began telling Karin how unbelievable the experience was—the weekend had an obvious and powerful impact on those kids.

Karin caught my excitement and joined my efforts. Together, we spent the next ten years teaching at that camp. We worked hard year after year to improve our workshops, but eventually, it wasn't enough, and we grew frustrated. We knew that we needed to be offering something more than just elk hunting techniques. We wanted our campers to experience the outdoors, learn about conservation, and catch the sacredness of taking an animal's life. We wanted to go deeper and offer an even more meaningful experience, so we began putting together a list of what that kind of camp would include:

- family values
- beginning each day with the Pledge of Allegiance
- prayer before every meal
- hunting instruction, good choices, and consequences
- kindness, support, and self-worth
- outdoor ethics and conservation
- leadership development
- social skills and communication

To make a long story short, in 2013, we filed for our own nonprofit license, and a few months later, Raised at Full Draw (RAFD) was born. To be honest, RAFD is my passion but also my blind spot. At times I have wanted RAFD to succeed so badly that I have allowed myself to make foolish and painful mistakes. Just as I made a poor decision while facing the elk that day in the Judith Mountains of Montana, I have made similar mistakes in my life outside of hunting—especially when it comes to our hunting camps.

One instance immediately comes to mind. A good friend called to ask if we could hold a RAFD camp in his hometown. Our camps had been in operation for about three years, and we had two camps up and going. There were plenty of red flags concerning his request, and my gut was telling me to say no. But I didn't want to disappoint my friend, so I agreed.

Opening our first two camps, I had learned that if a camp was to be successful, we needed a very organized and detailed plan of action. We needed to clearly define a list of benchmarks before opening a new camp. I explained to my friend the level of excellence necessary to open a safe and cost-effective camp. He agreed to my expectations and promised the new camp would be perfect in every aspect.

We were one month out, and after checking the registration, I began questioning my decision. Only 15 of the 50 kids we needed had signed up. I had been clear that we needed to have the camp at least half-full one month before the starting date, but here we were with only 30 days to go and only a fraction of the kids necessary. I wasn't sure what to do. I could tell my friend to cancel the camp and risk losing his friendship, or I could give the go-ahead and pray for a miracle. As I said, RAFD is my blind spot, so I decided to move forward. The miracle I prayed for never came. The camp was poorly attended; it even had several issues that put us at risk for losing all our camps.

Once again, I had decided based on what I had wanted, not on what was best. Now that the camp was over, I was faced with another decision, and this time I decided to make the right one by not returning to that camp. By doing so, I lost one of my dearest friends. As with the elk, I couldn't undo the damage I'd done, but I could learn from my mistake and make better decisions in the future—and that's exactly what I did.

With the elk and with my friend, I should have been ready to "let down." I should have done what my gut was telling me in both instances. You will find yourself in similar situations. There will be times when the opportunity you've been waiting for is at your fingertips, but remember, not every opportunity is good. If it doesn't feel right, chances are, it's not.

A group of Raised at Full Draw campers doing what they do best—having fun on the archery range and shooting, shooting, shooting...

INSTANT GROUND BLIND

It's hard to kill a buck if you don't blend in.

I don't know about you, but when someone talks about the month of November around my house, it conjures up one image. All I can imagine is a giant whitetail buck walking toward me on a crisp morning. For most bowhunters, that image is from the perspective of a tree stand. I love hunting from a tree stand, but there is something to be said about sitting on the ground at eye level in a hunting blind.

Ground blind hunting can be your secret weapon in taking the buck you're after, especially if you're in a spot where the right tree for hanging a stand isn't available. If you don't have a blind in your deer-hunting arsenal, you need to get one. Hunting from the ground is not only effective but also very affordable.

After years of trial and error with ground blinds, Karin and I have learned a few tricks along the way.

Blind hunting gives you the opportunity to hunt in areas with lots of deer traffic but no place to put a tree stand. Places like thickets and field edges. Blind hunting also allows you to hunt more comfortably in any weather condition.

Now, I'm going to let you in on a little secret that not only works but also makes blind hunting very cost-effective. I call it the pallet method. Hunting is an expensive hobby, and if you're like most hunters, you don't have an unlimited budget. It can be difficult to afford a hunting blind for every location you're planning on hunting. When you have to take the time to brush a blind in, the last thing you want to do is tear it down after every hunt. Years ago, I discovered a way around this problem, and it really works!

All you need are three pallets and three T-posts. I've never had to buy a pallet—most of the time you can find a local store that will give them away. Grocery or hardware stores are great places to start. Simply make a three-sided square with your pallets, leaving the front open. Drive a T-post through the center of each pallet, creating a permanent little fort. The next time you show up to hunt that spot, just drop in your blind, and you're ready to hunt. The deer won't even notice you're there because they are used to seeing the pallets in that spot. If you want to get a little more creative and make your full-time deer bunker a bit taller, you can slide a few limbs in the top of the pallets. Either way, it's cheap and super effective. I currently have about ten pallet sets. All I need is one ground blind—which I can easily take in and out—to hunt those spots. When you factor in the wind blowing from the right direction, you've got a great chance of catching your buck off guard from off the ground.

DAVID'S FAITH TIP

Let It Down or Let It Fly

Have you ever felt as if you've let God down? I'm guessing you've experienced that feeling more than once. I know I have. What frustrates me the most isn't the initial experience of letting God down—it's the repeating of that letdown. It's when I do what I said I would never do…and then do it again.

I've always considered my childhood to be mostly normal. My parents practiced balanced discipline, and I never felt as if they were too strict. However, as far back as I can remember, I watched them argue and fight. It was never physical fighting, but it did get extremely heated. Things were often said that I didn't understand and should have never heard as a kid. As a result, I began to formulate a plan for my own family—I would never argue with my wife like that, especially in front of our children. As great as that all sounds, I didn't consider that in order to turn my intentions into reality, I would need God's help.

Karin and I are now happily married, but it hasn't always been that way. We have had the same kind of heated battles my parents had—and in front of Warren and Easton. I will go one step further and admit that I have even had my share of similar battles with our boys. It's difficult for me to admit this, especially in a book for the world to read, but it is the truth.

I wish I could tell you that once I started pursuing a Christ-centered life, all that immediately went away, but that would be untrue. In fact, I sometimes look at other families who seem to get along effortlessly, and I wish I could be a fly on the wall. I often wonder what they're doing to make family life so seamless. But then I remember that they are human too and are no doubt going through struggles of their own.

The good news is, I believe the Lord is helping me and will help you too. But you have to let Him help, and the first step is to simply ask. Once you've asked, you will need to pay attention to how He has arranged to help you. Help could come from a friend, your pastor, or maybe just a gut feeling that you haven't been listening to. This book can help as well. I have found that God helps me most when I'm willing to give Him every aspect of my life. When I hold back, believing I can handle something on my own, I usually end up feeling like I've disappointed God, myself, and those around me. In the same way that you train to be an ultimate hunter, train yourself to be an ultimate believer, spouse, parent, and friend by including God in the details of your everyday life.

Begin to see yourself living at full draw, when your bow is pulled back and you are about to release an arrow at life, marriage, and parenting. If something feels off, don't do what I have done and risk a bad shot. Don't be afraid to "let down." You will be glad you did. God will lead you to other adventures, and this time when you shoot, your arrow will find its perfect mark. You too can go from "let it fly" to "let it down."

> *I do not understand what I do. For what I want*
> *to do I do not do, but what I hate I do.*
> **ROMANS 7:15**

> *What a wretched man I am! Who will rescue me from*
> *this body that is subject to death? Thanks be to God,*
> *who delivers me through Jesus Christ our Lord!*
> **ROMANS 7:24-25**

———— ENCOURAGEMENT FROM KARIN ————

No Trespassing

> *You were dead in your trespasses and sins.*
> **EPHESIANS 2:1 NASB**

We who hunt know the sinking feeling of pulling up to a property where we've previously hunted and seeing a new No Trespassing sign. It's frustrating not knowing who put the sign there or whether it applies to you. You know you should contact the landowner to see if the property has changed hands, but you also don't want to risk losing your favorite hunting spot. As landowners ourselves, David and I have had many people come onto our property without permission, and in some instances, they weren't even aware of the fact they were trespassing.

In Iowa, morel mushroom hunting is a big deal. Until we moved here, I had no idea that was even a thing. Morel mushrooms are delicious and can sell for up to $80 a pound. Who knew? Anyway, in the spring of the year, we sometimes come across a stranger who has wandered onto our property by accident, looking for those little treasures.

Most mushroom hunters mean well and aren't looking for a profit—they're just looking for their dinner! However, we occasionally encounter someone who believes that if we aren't going to pick the mushrooms, they are entitled to them even if it means trespassing onto our property. In my view, that's taking something that doesn't belong to you, and it is not okay. Besides, we are a family of hunters, and we often practice using our weapons. Even though we do this in the safest manner possible, the last thing we want is for someone to walk by at the wrong time and be injured.

We have no issue with someone hunting mushrooms on our land when they ask permission and follow the rules.

I think picking mushrooms on someone else's land, in many ways, is like your relationship with God. I know that may seem a bit far-fetched to you, but I see a spiritual connection in most everything we do outdoors. Consider these examples:

- Just like David and I need everyone on our property to abide by simple rules for their safety, God is also asking you to follow simple rules. Rules that He designed to keep you safe from the stray bullets of the world. Yet as humans, we struggle with this daily. I know I do. Jesus warned us about the danger of going off-road.

Small is the gate and narrow the road that leads to life, and only a few find it.
MATTHEW 7:14

- When someone trespasses on our land, my instinct is to feel as if they have violated and taken advantage of me. I want to be harsh with them and make it clear that they are never to return. I am grateful that God doesn't treat me like I sometimes want to treat others. I have this promise:

> *If we confess our sins, he is faithful*
> *and just and will forgive us our sins and*
> *purify us from all unrighteousness.*
> **1 JOHN 1:9**

- Because of God's forgiveness, I am learning to be more forgiving. Daily I must remind myself what the Scripture says:

> *Bear with each other and forgive one another*
> *if any of you has a grievance against someone.*
> *Forgive as the Lord forgave you.*
> **COLOSSIANS 3:13**

Forgiving someone like God forgave you is never easy, but if you are willing to do that, you can walk away from the situation with peace in your heart. Even when clear boundaries have been crossed, forgiveness is possible because of His cross.

REFLECTION

Has someone trespassed against you? How will you move forward now that the boundaries have been broken?

> *To be a Christian means to forgive the inexcusable*
> *because God has forgiven the inexcusable in you.*
> **C.S. LEWIS**

3

COMMUNICATION IS KEY

How to Effectively Use Game Calls

Many hunters have never experienced the feeling or the emotion that comes with using a game call to manipulate a wild animal into shooting range. I think it's because they're afraid of doing it wrong. They believe if they blow a call or smack a set of antlers together, every animal within hearing distance will instantly recognize the situation as a setup and hightail it out of there.

I have the gift of gab. And as I much as I love talking to people, I enjoy talking to animals even more. I am convinced a spiritual connection occurs when a hunter communicates with God's creation. Nothing is more exciting than enticing an animal to change its course, and if you're lucky, that animal might just end up right in your lap!

Unfortunately, just like conversations with my family don't always go as planned, my communication with an animal that happens to be on our "hit list" doesn't always translate well. Despite my best intentions, what I'm trying to say both in the woods and in the kitchen isn't always what is being heard.

I remember one deer season when Karin and I watched as deer

began pouring into a bean field. That was the good news. The bad news was we didn't have permission to hang a deer stand in the timber directly in front of them. I reassured Karin that we didn't need to get ahead of them because we could call them across the field to where we were sitting. I gave Karin some brief instructions, telling her to whack the antlers together on my signal, which she did perfectly. (This is called "rattling" and is one of the techniques we use to lure a white-tail buck into bow range.)

To our surprise, not one, but all the bucks immediately exited the field. That's when Karin gave me a look that said, "What in the world did we just communicate to those deer? Because whatever it was, they didn't like it at all." I wasn't sure what to say to her. It wasn't like I had anticipated all the deer getting out of there as fast as possible. And to be honest, to this day, I still don't know what went wrong. After an experience like that, you might be tempted to stop trying to speak to a buck by rattling antlers—believing that you will get the same negative reaction. But not me. I have seen rattling work time and time again. Just because Karin and I had one bad encounter with those deer, it doesn't mean that history will repeat itself. An ultimate hunter isn't rattled by a buck that doesn't respond to rattling.

Knowing when to call and when to just sit quietly can be difficult even for an experienced hunter. When Karin and I saw the bucks in the bean field, we had to call. It was our only chance to harvest one of those deer. But there will be other times when you will need to pay attention to what is going on in the woods around you and not call. I learned that lesson the hard way.

I had the opportunity to hunt an eight-point deer we call Juice. Warren and Easton gave him that name when they saw a huge jump in the size of his antlers from one year to the next. They joked that the only way he could have put on all those extra inches of bone was to take steroids! At the time, Juice was five years old and one of the bucks on my list of shooters. I had several encounters with him that season, but the first one was the most memorable. I often refer to that hunt as the day Juice got away.

My cameraman and I had just climbed into the tree stand, and before we could even get our equipment ready, deer were coming down the nearby trail, making their predawn exit from a cornfield. We tried to finish getting ready, but the deer just kept coming. It was getting light enough to film, and we could see several deer following the same path. Every deer in the woods was walking 20 yards from our stand, but so far, none were shooters.

Then suddenly my cameraman turned and said, "Big buck! Really big buck on the fence line."

I lifted my binoculars and saw Juice about 80 yards away. He was wearing out an overhanging cedar tree with his massive rack. I knew there was a good chance he would jump the fence and follow the same path all the other deer had used that morning. But in the back of my mind, I was also thinking, *What if he keeps heading down the fence line and disappears forever?*

I panicked. I decided that I needed to ignore the fact that all other deer had walked right past my stand. At that moment, I believed I needed to say something to Juice. I would let my rattling horns do the talking. I knew that nine out of ten times, a buck will head downwind to check the scent of the bucks he believes are fighting, and then he'll join the battle. If this was the case with Juice, I would have him at less than 30 yards in no time.

I smacked my antlers together and immediately got his attention. Juice raised his head and looked in my direction. Not wanting to overdo it, I rattled for only a few seconds. I didn't want Juice to zero in on my location, but I did need him to close the short gap between us. It worked! He jumped the fence and stood at less than 60 yards. But instead of coming straight at me as I had anticipated, he was veering off to the east to get downwind of the bucks he thought he had just heard fighting. To make matters worse, the wind that morning was blowing at more than 25 miles per hour with gusts up to 40. The excessive wind shortened my shooting distance, and if he kept going, he would pass outside of my effective bow range.

Juice finally stopped long enough for me to measure the distance between us with my rangefinder. He was standing at 37 yards. Under good weather conditions, and on a deer that was not alert, I would normally take that shot. But this morning, I had already determined that anything more than 30 yards was off-limits. So I watched as Juice worked his way around us until he caught our scent—then the hunt was over.

Looking back, I never gave Juice the chance to commit to the trail the other deer had followed that morning. If I had, he would have walked to within 20 yards of my deer stand (without being anxious) because he believed there were other bucks in his area. Instead of calling to Juice, I should have paid more attention to what was happening with the other deer and allowed him to follow in their footsteps. Instead, I panicked and ruined my chance. I learned a lesson that morning. Maybe it's not what you say but when you say it that's most important. On this hunt, I should have said nothing at all.

A colossal trail camera photo of Juice, the one-eyed warrior.

DAVID'S LIFE TIP

It's Not What You Say—It's How You Say It

Saying the wrong thing at the wrong time to an animal while hunting is one thing, but when you bring that concept into your relationships with people, it has an entirely different meaning. I know there have been times in my life when what I said was correct, but what the other person heard was not at all what I had intended.

I remember one incident with our youngest son, Easton, when what I said and what he heard couldn't have been further apart. As I have expressed on many occasions, I'm not perfect. Through the wonders of editing, most of what you see on our show (*Raised Hunting*) has been polished, but I'm not as polished as you might think. I still describe myself as a bit of a redneck—I sometimes say or do things that others might not consider normal. For example, I have checked into the Ritz Carlton Hotel with a bow case in my hand, wearing camo shorts, a tank top, and Crocs. I have even been known to use the Jacuzzi tub in my hotel room as a washer for my hunting clothes and the railing on the balcony as a dryer. That's the real David Holder (much to his wife's dismay).

This context may help you understand what happened in my conversation with Easton. I don't remember exactly how the entire conversation went, but I do know that it had something to do with sports. I was trying to get Easton to understand that life is tough and that God sometimes allows us to face difficult situations so we can learn how to deal with them. Looking back, that's how I wish I had said it. I wanted Easton to toughen up and learn how to stand up for himself so life wouldn't squish him like a bug. Easton, who was ten years old at the time, thought I was calling him wimpy, and I ended up hurting him more than I had helped. The problem wasn't what I had said; it was how I had said it.

That experience with Easton taught me something valuable. Just as I need to be careful and pay attention when I'm communicating with the animals we hunt, I need to be mindful of what I say to the people God has placed in my life. I'm slowly learning that words are like toothpaste. Once it's out of the tube, it's impossible to put it back. If I had only taken the time to better explain myself, the entire situation could have been avoided and my size-ten foot would have stayed out of my size-five mouth!

I'll give you one more example. This situation was like the one with Juice—I should have said nothing at all. Karin and I were newlyweds, and she wanted to start a new Thanksgiving tradition. She decided that instead of turkey, mashed potatoes and gravy, stuffing, and all the trimmings, she would do a Thanksgiving quiche. Since the holidays are packed with several large meals, Karin thought it would be nice to cut back by fixing something simple yet delicious. That was fine with me, but I assumed she would be serving other dishes as well. I mean, you don't have eggs without bacon or sausage. And you certainly don't have toast without butter or jam, right? So when Karin brought out the quiche, my natural question was, Where is the rest of Thanksgiving dinner?

All the color drained out of Karin's face, and for the first time in my life, I saw flames in her eyes! At that moment, I realized that I should have kept my comments to myself and said nothing about the disappointment I felt when the only thing on the table was a single pan. Don't get me wrong—the quiche was incredible, and I told her so, but it was too late. Karin was very upset and wanted to know why I didn't care that she had worked hard to prepare that quiche for me. Now on Thanksgiving, we joke about that quiche (as we eat turkey and stuffing), but at the time, it was not a joke—at least not to Karin.

The point I'm trying to make is that at one time or another, whether in the woods or in the kitchen, all of us have said something that we shouldn't have. In a moment of inattention, we blurted out the wrong thing by not giving thought to how it would be received. In those instances, all we can do is apologize and take the lesson to heart so we don't repeat our behavior.

Mistakes are opportunities to learn and grow into the person you want to become. Believe it or not, mistakes can actually make you a better hunter and a better person.

These days, I think before I speak, and I do my very best to make sure that what comes out of my mouth will benefit the people in my life. That doesn't mean I tiptoe around difficult issues. It just means I'm learning when to keep my mouth closed—especially when it's full of quiche!

DAVID'S FAITH TIP

Prayer Is What You Say to God

Please, God, just let that buck walk over here, and I promise I will be a better Christian. I will do whatever You ask me to do—just let me kill this deer.

Does that prayer sound familiar? Those words often sum up the prayer life of every Christian bowhunter when the buck of a lifetime is walking by just out of range. You can get "spiritual" in a hurry when you believe you might not get a shot.

I've been guilty of praying only when I wanted or needed something from God. I've stopped in the middle of a stressful situation to ask God for help...even though three months had passed since I had taken the time to bow my head to be thankful for a delicious meal.

Imagine what it would be like if you and I stopped treating God like a wishing well. What if God became more than just a place to go when we wanted Him to do something for us? As I've said before, there was a time in my life when God was my backup plan. If I couldn't figure out the answer on my own, I would go to Him as a last resort. And even though it's taken me a while to figure this out, I'm now learning how to go to God as my first option and not my last. I now realize that the answers I'm looking for aren't based on what I can do for myself but on what only God can do for me. By doing this, God is blessing me every day and not just showing up as a lifeguard on the days I feel as if I'm drowning.

God is no longer my wishing well. He is my leader.

Karin often points out that I talk to animals better than I talk to people—and she's right. Speaking to animals is easy because I have a clear message that I'm trying to convey. I am saying to them, "Hey, come over here. I promise I'm real." At that moment, I am totally focused on what I am saying, and I'm listening to the animal's response.

I try very hard to bring that same focus into my prayer life. When I call out to God, I'm both talking to Him and listening to His response. You can call out to God as well. He is listening, and just like the animals you hunt, He will draw near to you when you call out to Him.

TAKE CARE OF THE MEAT

You can't eat it if it's spoiled.

Being a good hunter isn't just about the preparation that goes into the harvesting of an animal. Many hours go into a hunt before a single arrow is released or the roar of a muzzle blast echoes through the timber. Getting ready to hunt is essential, but I've always taught that what you do *after* you have punched your tag is equally important.

The goal of every hunter should be to bring home the tasty reward of a successful hunt. It's the meat we value. How you approach skinning, storing, and packing your freshly killed animal will determine how much of that animal you can safely eat. For example, with the invention of airtight super coolers, you might be tempted to believe you don't need as much ice as in the old days. However, if you don't layer the ice between every piece of meat, your game can still spoil in a very short time. This is a lesson I learned the hard way.

A few years ago, we killed and quartered a big bull elk. Rather than taking the time to bone-out the meat, we just laid the quarters in a cooler. Then we filled all the crevices and the top with ice. I thought everything was fine...until we got to the meat processor. Upon inspecting the meat, the butcher informed me that the entire cooler of elk was spoiled. I was shocked and asked him what he was talking about. He showed me that the meat on top was ice cold, but since the cooler was airtight and we had filled it so fully, no cool air was able to get to the bottom. Basically, the meat on top acted like an oven, spoiling all the meat below. We had done all that work, and because of a stupid mistake on my part, we lost everything. The moral of the story is, always ice meat from the bottom to the top and between layers.

The other mistake we made that day was not boning-out the elk. When you bone-out an animal, you release the heat trapped inside the meat, causing it to stay fresh longer. In addition, the butcher weighed more than 100 pounds of useless bones! That was something my back and legs did not appreciate hearing. Now we never skip this important step.

I'll add one last tip that will help you keep more of your kill. If you're going to quarter and bone-out an animal, don't gut it. Not gutting a big-game animal saves time and energy. By starting the boning process sooner, the chances of losing any of your prize are greatly decreased, and you're less likely to contaminate your meat by accidentally cutting into the guts.

For a full demonstration video on how to best utilize the gutless method, download our Raised Outdoors app and look in the field care section.

*Call to me and I will answer you and tell you great
and unsearchable things you do not know.*

JEREMIAH 33:3

ENCOURAGEMENT FROM KARIN

Listening to God Speak

"I can't hear him," I whispered to David and Warren.

It was early September in the mountains of Montana, yet it felt like July with temperatures soaring into the nineties. David, Warren, and I were bowhunting for elk. Apparently, there was a bull bugling in a nearby deep drainage ditch, but I couldn't hear him. David, however, had pinpointed his location and was motioning for Warren and me to follow him to the bull. In our rush to get there, sprinting across a field and several ridges, we became overheated. By the time we had reached the drop-off, we were all breathing hard and trying to hold our breath just long enough to hear the bull bugle one more time, giving away his exact location.

"Hear that?" David asked. I could tell by the intense, excited look on Warren's face that he too could hear the bull. David then took out a cow call and made an invitational sound that only a bull elk could be drawn to.

On this hunt, I was the shooter, Warren was the cameraman, and David was the caller. David's job was to call the bull past me so I could take the shot. Elk are super keen, with bionic-like senses, so it's important that the caller not be sitting right beside the shooter. This increases your odds by keeping the bull's attention away from the archer hiding in the brush. When elk hunting, every team member must be in sync. So if one of us can't hear the bull, it's a major issue. Needless to say, we had a major issue that day, as I still could not hear this bull bugling.

Astonished and more than a bit annoyed, David looked at me and said, "Karin, how can you not hear that bugle? He is literally right over the ridge!"

How can I not hear that? I've often wondered the same thing many times in my life—and not just while elk hunting. As I was trying to figure out how to answer David's question, I noticed all the barriers keeping me from hearing the bull: the wind blowing, my hard breathing, the ridge blocking some of the sounds, and the hearing loss that comes with being in your forties. Those are legit excuses…unlike all the noise and negative self-talk that was going on in my head.

Just like on that elk hunt, there have been many times in my life when I have wondered, *Lord, how come I can't hear You?* I've even asked, *God, are You there? Can You hear me? Are You distracted with all the other issues of the world? Have You forgotten about little old me?* But then I remember one of my favorite Scriptures.

> *Every good and perfect gift is from above,*
> *coming down from the Father of the heavenly lights,*
> *who does not change like shifting shadows.*
> **JAMES 1:17**

The book of James clearly states that God is unchanging. And that can only mean one thing: I am the one who is coming and going—not God. I'm the one who sometimes disconnects like a shifting shadow, depending on my circumstances. I'm now realizing that if I want to hear God's voice, I have to push out all the negative noise and just be present in the conversation. I can hear God when I position myself correctly.

Now back to the hunt…

David had quickly moved into action and had dropped over the hill behind us in order to get completely out of the bull's line of sight. He was still calling in order to keep the bull elk interested in the pretty lady elk he was looking for. Warren was frantically setting up the camera and trying to get tucked away under a nearby cedar bush. "Get ready, Mom," he said. "He is coming! Get an arrow ready *now*."

The moment had finally arrived. What I had been dreaming and praying about for years was now staring me in the face. My heart was pumping so hard and fast that I thought it would flop out of my chest at any moment. I looked up and saw the most magnificent bull elk I had ever laid eyes on. He was surrounded by a harem of cows and was walking directly toward me. I knew if he stayed on the trail, he would walk by at about 30 yards. I had prayed for a good bull, but this was more than I had hoped for. The barriers no longer mattered as he was now so close that I could smell him. He stopped. I took aim and watched as my arrow hit the bull. I knew the placement was less than perfect, so I prayed, *Please, Lord, let the arrow do its job.*

Warren was intently watching where the bull had gone, and David was now approaching over the hill from where he had been calling. I dreaded telling him I thought the shot was bad. I didn't want to disappoint my husband, and not getting a clean kill on one of God's creatures was even worse.

I had hit the bull too far back, and after days of tracking, we did not recover him.

REFLECTION

Do you have barriers keeping you from hearing God's voice? What one thing will you do today to help remove those barriers?

My grace is sufficient for you, for my power is made perfect in weakness.

2 CORINTHIANS 12:9

4

BE PREPARED

Preparing Yourself for a Hunt

I'm often asked when I start preparing for a hunt. My answer is always the same. I never *start* preparing to hunt because I never *stop* preparing. As a matter of fact, as I write this chapter, I'm focusing on my next hunt. That's how obsessed I truly am. I think that every day is an opportunity to prepare for the next day—not just with hunting but also in life. I believe that paying attention to details and always being prepared helps me succeed.

Preparation means something different to each of us, and when it comes to hunting, I don't know if we are ever fully prepared to participate in something so sacred as the taking of an animal's life. All we can do is give it our best.

For example, when I plan a whitetail hunt, I don't just pick a stand location in the general area. I consider the deer sign, wind direction, and other key factors, and then I strategically choose the spot that I believe will give me the best chance of success. So I scout nonstop. Anytime I am in the woods, I am constantly watching for anything that could tip me off to a new spot or even a new idea. I check trails, creek crossings, and fences. I watch how deer enter and exit the crops in the area. I even plant my own crops to tip the scale in my favor.

In 2018, I experienced a deer season that perfectly illustrates the importance of scouting and using information gathered over time to make a hunt successful. The year before, my video team and I were getting ready to burn off the overgrown grass on a piece of our property, but I suggested that we first walk through a brushy area to check for shed antlers before we started the burn. Reluctantly, they agreed to enter the timbered mess of thorns and sapling trees.

We never found a shed, but we did find what would become my new stand location for this area. As we walked the heavily worn trail through the thicket, I came across the kind of deer rub every hunter has dreamed about. This rub was the size of my thigh! And there was more than one. As I approached the rub, I realized that it was not your ordinary, run-of-the-mill rub. The deer using this tree to polish his antlers had been there many times over the span of a few years. I had found what I call a signpost rub. This kind of rub isn't one that a deer quickly forgets about after stopping to clean the velvet off his antlers. A signpost rub is usually located on a large tree and can even appear to have an hourglass shape as one or more bucks are constantly giving it a good lashing over a long period of time. A rub like this is usually dark from years of wear and not bright yellow from fresh scarring.

I don't often find rubs like this, but when I do, I take note. And even though bow season was still eight months away, I knew that by going into the thick brush looking for sheds, I had found something even better. I had found a "honey hole." As we studied and filmed the rub, I began the process of planning how I would hunt this little gold mine.

When placing a stand in thick brush, I look for the trees best suited to give me a view of the area. I also note which direction I will need the deer to pass by without noticing that I have invaded their turf. In this brushy area, I was getting discouraged by the lack of trees to pick from. The largest trees were the ones the deer were rubbing on. Just as I was about to give up hope, I looked up the hill and saw a cluster of tangled vines and thorns encompassing a large cedar tree. I couldn't possibly get a deer stand in there, but I could tuck a blind in the brush, giving me a 20-yard shot. I was determined to get this spot ready.

I returned several weeks before the opening of bow season to place a trail camera. I felt so confident, even before getting one picture of a possible shooter buck, that I cut a walking path and set up a blind in the tangled mess beneath the cedar tree I had found earlier. All I needed now was for the season to open, and I would be in business.

It seemed like an eternity, but bow season finally came. I was getting a few trail camera pictures of some really nice bucks. I hadn't seen anything huge yet, but there were some shooters. After seeing signs that the rut was kicking in, a cold front also passed through the area, giving me the north wind I had been waiting for. My cameraman and I slipped into the blind that morning without making a sound. By previously cutting a walking path, we had avoided the heavily used trail the deer were taking. I had taken everything into account, and as the darkness gave way to morning light, I could see that the cluster of rubs in front of us had been freshly marked.

I was pumped. Everything seemed perfect as the wind was blowing straight in our faces. But I'm also a seasoned hunter, and I know things don't always play out the way we have envisioned them. So I was somewhat surprised when my cameraman tapped my leg and whispered, "Buck, buck, buck." All the scouting and preparation were coming together in an instant.

The buck walked to the first rub and began moving his forehead up and down the tree. He took his time as if he was signing his name. All I could do was watch as the heavy-horned ten-pointer wore out the tree 15 yards in front of me. My heart was pounding, and my mouth went dry as the buck faced me. I had no shot. Suddenly, he turned and started to walk to the next tree. He was now broadside at 13 yards. When I released the arrow, I saw my lighted nock disappear behind his shoulder.

When a buck of that size is on the ground in front of me, I experience an adrenaline jolt that takes a while to recover from. Once my head was clear, all I could think about was how this moment had started almost a year ago from a fluke shed hunt that had turned into a scouting trip. All those months of preparation had paid off as the big buck was piled up not far from where I had shot him.

Paying attention to the smallest of details can lead us all to big rewards. David sits with his 2018 Iowa buck.

Paying close attention to the smallest of details had worked, and it can work for you as well. Just remember to always be looking, open to learning, and ready to gather information. You never know what might come of all that preparation. If you're lucky, it just might be a bill from your taxidermist.

EFFECTIVELY USING DEER DECOYS

Take one antler off.

When it comes to using deer decoys, there seems to be no middle ground. Either you love them or you've never used them. Most whitetail hunters see decoys as a huge hassle—big, bulky, and not guaranteed to work. I will admit that I can't argue with any of that. However, if you want an unbelievable encounter with the most sought-after quarry in North America (the white-tail buck), place a decoy by your stand.

Every whitetail hunter knows that setup is the most impor-tant element in every hunt. How you approach a hunting situa-tion is more important than the kind of calls you use or the type of bow you shoot. Your decoy setup is no different. If you want decoy hunting to work, you have to get it right. I've learned a few pointers that I hope will help you bag the big one.

The first question you have to ask yourself is, *Do I need a doe or buck decoy?* The answer depends on the time of the season. The only time I use a doe decoy is when the breeding season is dwindling and the bucks have started to run out of does. In my experience, if a buck sees a doe decoy late in the breeding sea-son, he will usually come to check her out. The rest of the time, I use a buck decoy—especially right before and during the rut.

You may wonder, *Why use a decoy at all? How come I can't just set up in the right area and wait until a big boy comes stroll-ing by?* The truth is, you can. But it's not always that easy, espe-cially when bowhunting. If your buck is always 20 yards out of range, it can be very frustrating. This is where decoy hunting can give you a huge advantage—by putting that big buck right in your lap.

Once you decide to give decoy hunting a try, the next step is understanding the list of dos and don'ts. In my opinion, it is not wise to use a two-dimensional decoy when bowhunting. Two-dimensional decoys were designed for a hunter to hide behind and don't work when an animal approaches from the side. I always pick the most realistic three-dimensional decoy I can find and afford. I like decoys that have some movement in the head or tail, are easy to set up and tear down, and yet have lifelike features.

Lastly, I implement my best trick—taking off one of the ant-lers and sticking it in my backpack. You might ask, *Why on earth would he do that?* I take off an antler because it shows a weakness, and deer know that a weakness in an opponent increases their chance of winning. If they see a one-antlered buck, you can be assured they will come to that buck from the weak side.

I set my buck decoys 15 to 20 yards straight upwind from my location with the head facing me. Bucks tend to approach other bucks head-on. They approach does from the rear, so I would set up a doe decoy in the same place but facing straight or quartering away from me, ensuring the best shot angle. I never set my decoys far away because a deer will come directly to another deer or circle a few yards away. I also try to avoid touching my decoys with my bare hands. Wearing gloves is your best bet. Lastly, I use some sort of glandular scent just underneath the decoy to add one more element of realism.

Even though we have just scratched the surface on decoying deer, I promise you if you ever try it and see it work, you will be asking yourself why you didn't do this long before. Yes, decoys are extra work, but when you start telling your buddies about the raging buck that pounded your decoy into the dirt or launched it high into the air, you will be ready to drag it out again next year.

DAVID'S LIFE TIP

Preparing Yourself for Parenting

You probably know how to prepare for your next hunt, but how do you prepare for life? To be honest, I'm not sure you can, at least not all at once. You can ready yourself for certain things at certain times. And how you do that will have a huge impact on how well you move forward or if you move forward at all. More than once, I have failed to prepare properly and had to watch as my hopes and expectations crumbled right before my eyes. However, I've also had those instances where careful preparation and planning have paid off.

The most memorable example of *not* being prepared for life that I can think of was my plan for a family. Neither of our boys were "perfectly" planned on, nor were they a complete "whoops." Karin and I just kind of left that in God's hands. I remember the day Karin told me she was pregnant with Warren and how that day changed our world forever. I had always wanted kids, and I would have been happy with boys or girls. All I could envision was taking them hunting and fishing with me. I wanted to teach them everything I knew about the outdoors. I felt prepared and qualified to pass on my love for all things outside. But like all first-time dads, there were plenty of other things I was *not* prepared for when it came to raising children.

Warren Paul Holder was born December 28, 1995, ten days after his due date. After Warren's birth, I became a different man. For the next two years, life was all about diapers, late nights, and countless hours of watching him do just about anything. As much as I loved those early days, something special happened about the time Warren turned three years old—my son became my best friend. Now he could walk, talk, and tell me what he wanted to eat, let me know if something was hurting him, and (thankfully!) use the bathroom on his own.

The best part was, he could talk his mom into letting us spend more time outside looking for deer or shooting our bows. I had no doubt that even at an early age, Warren would inherit my passion for hunting. He lived for shooting his bow and was a menace to the local gopher population. He loved to fish, and even though he wouldn't touch a worm, he would fish with me everywhere I went. I loved watching him grow and feel his way through life. But what I loved most was how he and I were truly best friends.

In 2000, we added a new best friend to our little team: Easton David Holder. With an older brother to guide him, Easton learned everything Warren had learned, only faster. It wasn't long until the entire Holder family could be found at local archery shoots or at one of the various campgrounds in the heart of the Rockies, chasing tin cans with a BB gun or sitting around a campfire sharing s'mores. Without a doubt, those were the best years of my life. I had always loved spending time outside, and now I had an entire family to share my experiences. Our time together in some of God's most beautiful handiwork far surpassed any of the days I had spent outdoors by myself. From the first gopher, to the first deer, to the first fish—I loved every second of it.

That's all well and good, but there were a lot of other things that happened while our boys were growing up that I wasn't prepared for. Like the time Warren stuck a stick in his eye and had to be taken to the emergency room. Or when Easton lost his driving privileges and had to ride the school bus. Good things eventually change or even come to an end. And while you seek to hang on to those moments from your past, sometimes all you can do is let go and allow God to move you into the next season of life. As my boys grew into young men, our relationships changed. We still enjoyed spending time together, but between our outings, we began arguing about cars, girls, curfews, and grades.

I often thought about what it would be like to have kids, but I didn't spend much time thinking about what it would be like once they were grown and gone. I remember the day my best friend, Warren, came to me and said it was time for him to move out on his own. As awful as that day was, it only got worse. A few years later, my other best friend, Easton, graduated high school, and he also moved. Suddenly, just like on the days they were born, I was once again a different man. Only this time it wasn't for the better—or so I thought, as I would have to learn to navigate in a world without daily interaction with them. My boys were now adult men, and I was left with an empty feeling that I wasn't prepared for.

Before Warren and Easton were born, I had spent a good portion of my life preparing for the days we would spend together and how I would make the most of them. But in my excitement, I had forgotten to prepare for the day when all that would end. I never even considered what it would be like when they would move out on their own or that there would be a time when they would want to share the outdoors with their own families and friends.

Honestly, those early days had gone by so fast that I didn't even know if I had done my job as their dad. Had I prepared them for life? Had I given them the tools they needed to one day become good dads themselves? When something ends before you're ready, I think it is human nature to be critical of yourself by giving more attention to what you wish you had done, rather than focusing on all the good things you did. I now look back at certain conversations that I wish I had handled more delicately or said something more effectively. I can't go back and change my mistakes, but I do believe that I did my best, I also learned a few things the hard way, and I'm happy to pass those along to you.

Never take a day with your family for granted. Cherish that moment every morning when the sun touches their faces, because it will be gone in an instant. Hold tightly to that little hand when it softly grabs for yours. Squeeze a little tighter and a little longer when they shoot their first deer or catch their first fish. Run your fingers through their hair a little slower when they lay their head on your lap as you drive home.

Believe me when I tell you that you can do a lot more to prepare yourself for the day they enter your life than you can for the day they step out of it. Treasure every moment, even when it is tough. You won't regret it.

DAVID'S FAITH TIP

Preparing for a Relationship with the Savior

I can prepare to hunt, work, and even spend time with my family. But how do I prepare myself to have a relationship with God? The answer is not as complicated as you might think.

I believe that everything I do—from giving instructions at one of our hunting camps to talking to the gas station attendant—should be done with the Lord in mind. In a nutshell, I believe that from the time I am born until the day I die, I should be preparing myself for a voyage to heaven by the way I live my life on the earth. I believe that faith in Jesus Christ isn't just *my* answer, but the answer for the entire world.

I will admit that I don't always live with heaven in mind, and I don't want you to read this and think that I'm the guy with all the answers, because I am not. I'm thankful that God has a system in place for imperfect people like me—a system that clearly says that because

I have given my life to Jesus and have placed my faith in Him, I now have my spot in God's kingdom.

As someone who has prepared for major moves, big hunts, and overwhelming challenges, I can say with certainty that God is offering you a great deal—one you don't want to miss out on! It's quite simple. All He asks is that you live your life with Jesus as the center, and in exchange, you will receive eternal life.

But how do you build your life around Jesus? Not by arriving at your workplace on time every day or by hugging your kids and telling them you love them. It's not even about being a great husband or a dependable friend. Those are all great qualities, but our goodness doesn't get us into heaven. It's Jesus—nothing more and nothing less.

I realize that for some people, seeing is believing. If they find the right sign, they are confident they will kill a deer. But believing in things they can't see—such as God—is much more difficult. However, just like in scouting, there is evidence that God is there even if you've never laid your eyes on Him. Just as a buck rub tells that a buck is nearby, God has also left signpost rubs, ensuring me that even though I can't see Him, He is still close. If you're careful to scout for signs of God's existence, you won't have to look very far to see where He's been and what He's been up to.

A scarred-up tree may be able to tell you that a buck is close, but a scarred-up Savior hanging on a tree guarantees you that God is even closer.

Everyone who calls on the name of the Lord will be saved.
ROMANS 10:13

ENCOURAGEMENT FROM KARIN

Lessons from Martha

> Now as they went on their way, Jesus entered a village. And a woman named Martha welcomed him into her house. And she had a sister called Mary, who sat at the Lord's feet and listened to his teaching. But Martha was distracted with much serving. And she went up to him and said, "Lord, do you not care than my sister has left me to serve alone? Tell her then to help me." But the Lord answered her, "Martha, Martha, you are anxious and troubled about many things, but one thing is necessary. Mary has chosen the good portion, which will not be taken away from her" (Luke 10:38-42 ESV).

I find it easy to relate to Martha. I'm a doer. In my early years as a young mom, I thought the house had to be perfect when guests came over. Everything needed to be in its place. In fact, when we did have guests, I would fiddle around in the kitchen like Martha most of the time (probably because I am more comfortable working than socializing). I always loved the fact that David is a great socializer. He would pick up the slack when I was not really that into it.

Relationships, not properly fluffed pillows, mattered most to Jesus. Even though it's taken me a few years to realize this, I am working hard to be more like Mary.

We were living in Great Falls, Montana, when Warren turned 12. This meant he could now hunt with David and me. Anyone who knows Warren knows that he is as consumed with hunting as David is. It's in his blood.

On the opening Saturday of the 2007 deer season, David was out of town doing elk seminars for Primos Hunting and would not be home for a couple of days. As a career woman and mother, I used Saturdays to catch up on groceries, laundry, dusting, cleaning, walking the dog, and so on. I was hustling around doing all these things when Warren approached me and said, "Mom, it's opening day of deer season. Can we please go hunting?"

"Not today, Warren. I have too much housework to do," I replied.

Warren turned and walked away, but he showed up again ten minutes later. "Come on, Mom, it's opening day!"

Once again, I gave him a firm no. Warren left the room and went to play with Easton. I could tell that I had hurt his feelings and that he was more than disappointed with my answer.

That started a conversation in my head. *Why did I say no?* I asked myself.

Because David is not here, and you have never taken the boys hunting without him. And besides, you don't know what you're doing. That was the lie that had presented itself in my head.

That's when something rose up within me. I began to think, *Wait just a minute! I do know what I am doing. I have hunted for close to 15 years. I know where to go, how to get there, and how to field dress a deer. What am I waiting for?*

The dusting and the dishes can wait, but my son's first day of deer season only comes one time…ever!

"Warren!" I hollered. "Get your hunting clothes on, and grab your bow and your brother. Let's go hunting!"

I have never seen my son move so quickly in my entire life. I changed my clothes and grabbed a bag of snacks, and the three of us climbed into my Chevy Malibu (car!) and headed to our hunting property. We called David on the way. He was shocked—and sad that he couldn't be there to share the moment with us.

"How will you field dress it if you get one?" he asked.

"The same way you do," I replied.

"Where will you put it? You have a car."

"On the roof, I suppose."

The boys and I laughed at the thought of strapping a deer to the top of our car.

"Good luck," David said. "I hope you get one. I'm so proud of you guys."

Warren looked at me. "Thanks, Mom."

I now fully realize that the time we spend building relationships and connecting with our loved ones and with God is more precious than anything else we could be doing. The work can almost always wait. But the stopping and listening to others and Jesus can't. I'm so glad that Jesus gives me permission to sit at His feet and listen to Him.

REFLECTION

Do you have Martha moments? What can you change today to help you build the kind of relationship with Jesus that He desires?

5

HUNT THE WIND

Don't Let Them Smell You

Regardless of how high you hang your stand in a tree or how well you camouflage your ground blind, if you don't hunt the wind, you won't win. I've been known to walk for miles to get downwind from my quarry. Sometimes the only way to tip the odds in my favor is to take the long way. An ultimate hunter understands that you may be able to fool the eyes of most animals, but it's nearly impossible to fool their noses.

In my 40 years of hunting, I've learned a few simple characteristics that most big game animals share. If they see you but don't hear or smell you, they might not immediately run away. A big game animal will often study something they're not familiar with to see if perhaps you are a predator or if you're just another nonthreatening entity in their world.

For example, if you're just a rancher fixing fences, they might not consider you a threat and see no need to vacate the area. Don't get me wrong—you won't look like a barn or an abandoned piece of equipment left in a field that they walk past every day, so they will keep an eye on you. But they won't be too concerned unless your demeanor changes to that of a predator or something they've never seen. I've also noticed if an animal sees or hears me but can't tell what I am or what I am doing, that animal won't take a chance and will immediately bolt in search of a safer location.

An animal's sense of smell is, without a doubt, its best defense mechanism. If it can smell you in a place where you aren't normally supposed to be, such as the ridge it beds on or next to a field where it feeds, it doesn't need to see or hear you to be on high alert. Animals know what you are and where you are. Their instincts will kick in, and they will assume that you are a predator and up to no good. At that point, their only option is to leave the area.

That's why I teach in our seminars how critical it is to always hunt the wind. I know how tempting it can be to want to hunt your favorite stand location when the wind isn't in your favor, especially if you have a limited number of days to hunt. But oftentimes, I don't hunt in one of my favorite locations because the wind is blowing in the wrong direction. One of our hit-list bucks may be roaming in that area, but I won't risk it. It's just not worth it. When it comes to hunting really big elk or deer, you don't get multiple chances. Once they pick up on the fact that you are hunting them, they will change the game—and trust me, it's never changed in your favor.

Several years ago, I was hunting elk in the Missouri Breaks of Montana. At the time, I only had very limited elk hunting experience. I had successfully hunted this area before but not consistently. I decided to try a new tactic that morning. The creek bottom was filled with watering holes and plenty of food for the elk, so they would come from miles away to spend their nights gorging on the lush meadow grass. Then every morning at first light, the elk would start their long trek back to the timber, where they would spend the day resting. The elk followed this pattern day after day on a repeated loop.

In the past, I had always slipped into the creek bottom before daylight to try to get the attention of one of the bulls before the herd began its morning commute back to the timber. Today was going to be different because, in my mind, I was turning the table on the elk. Instead of hunting the elk in the creek bottom at first light, I had hiked my way into the timber they called home to set up. Now all I had to do was wait for them to return.

I thought my plan was foolproof. I knew that they came back here every morning and that once they were done frolicking in their little oasis, they would have full bellies and be ready to bed down. The wind was blowing perfectly out of the west, and the elk would be coming from straight north. All I had to do was be patient.

The plan was working perfectly, and about an hour after sunrise, I could hear the elk coming. Their high-pitched screaming filled the timber around me. At this point, they were still about a mile away, but I could see them through my binoculars. The first group of elk arrived, filling the drainage ditch 200 yards away. I would soon get my chance at one of those bulls. As the herd edged closer, I started thinking about how many trips it would take to pack my bull out of the remote timber.

My arrogant thoughts were short-lived as I glanced over my shoulder just in time to catch a small bull on high alert. He was standing on a ridge straight east of where I was sitting. My first thought was, *Okay, I haven't moved, so I know he doesn't see me. But why is he so alert?* Then I felt it…the wind hit the back of my neck. My second thought was, *Oh no. He is straight downwind.* After a few tense seconds, I finally calmed, telling myself not to worry because the herd was still coming. Suddenly, the small bull on the ridge was joined by another bull of about the same size. It was more than obvious that the two of them were having a major issue with something in the area.

What happened next is every elk hunter's worst nightmare. The two elk on the ridge 500 yards away began sounding a warning call. And they did it so many times that they finally gained the attention of the herd. The entire time I had been watching the alerted young bull and his buddy, the herd had been moving closer and closer to my location. So when the warning call went out, the herd was only 100 yards away. With one last loud bark, the two bulls on the ridge turned and trotted in the opposite direction.

I can see them still, with their noses high in the air as they crossed each flat and widened the distance quickly to more than a mile away.

I turned my attention back to the herd in front of me. They too had grown nervous from all the commotion. They had all the information they needed from their two buddies on the ridge to know that they weren't going to continue in my direction. I watched as the entire herd trotted off without ever coming close enough for a shot.

I sat there scratching my head and wondering what in the world had just happened. Could those two young bulls have smelled me from that far away? You bet they did! There was no other explanation for what had just happened. That day changed the way I hunt elk, and I decided to make it a priority to always do everything I can to control my scent—including switching all personal hygiene items such as soap and deodorant to the unscented brands. I even carry a change of hunting clothes in a no-scent Ziploc bag. All those things can certainly help, but they cannot eliminate all human odor—so when all else fails, hunt the wind.

--------------------- **DAVID'S LIFE TIP** ---------------------

Position Yourself for Success

Hunting the wind is more than simply a good idea, it's absolutely necessary if you want to enjoy a successful hunt. In my experience, when you don't pay attention to the direction your scent is blowing, you're only setting yourself up for a long, boring hunt. Once you settle this issue in your mind, hunting becomes easier and a lot less frustrating.

I've found that we must decide to live by certain principles or values in life—and we must refuse to waiver. When we follow those principles, our chances of success instantly increase. Whether we realize it or not, we are hunting the wind in our everyday lives. (I'm not talking about circling around the people at your work or school in order to get downwind of them. That would likely get you thrown into a psychiatric ward!)

Allow me to pose a question: What if hunting the wind means living within certain absolutes that you have decided will guide your life? Absolutes such as honesty, respect, integrity, responsibility, and believing in yourself. Just as I have decided not to hunt when the wind is wrong because my chances for success go way down, I have also decided not to participate in certain things that would decrease my chances of enjoying a successful life. I'm always hunting the wind. I do my best to position myself for success. I will admit that I've missed the mark more than once, but hey, that's life and hunting.

I've always considered myself a confident person. The trick is not allowing confidence to turn into arrogance. I think the difference between the two is easy to recognize. Confidence in your ability pushes you to do things that your mind and your body are telling you are impossible. Confidence is quietly believing in yourself. Arrogance, on the other hand, is broadcasting how fast, strong, and great you are. Arrogance is the loud promoting of yourself.

Karin and I have taught our boys that we never have to tell others how good we are at anything, and we've tried to live by that belief. If we're truly good at something and we're doing it for the right reasons, others will recognize our ability without us pointing it out. We've even gone one step further, emphasizing that it really doesn't matter what other people think anyway—the only standard we need to live up to is the standard we've set for ourselves.

When I was 27 years old, I tested for a new job with the Montana Fire Department. I will never forget that day. I sat in my hotel room on the phone with Karin. I was trying to explain to her that even though I had received a 96 percent on their exam and had four years of experience under my belt, I was still number 48 on their list of applicants. The fire department had awarded military preference points to veterans, and since I had never served in the armed forces, I was automatically forced to the bottom of the list. They were allowing only 50 candidates to compete the next day in the physical exam, which included running an obstacle course. Then they would take the top 20 candidates and interview them after looking at what they had scored on the written exam. This meant I needed 28 candidates to fail the physical exam in order to even have a chance to interview.

I explained to Karin that there was no point in going to the physical exam and that I had just wasted a lot of time and money—money that we didn't have. I was upset because in my mind, I had just driven across the country to take a test that didn't really matter. To say I was disappointed and angry would be an understatement. As I continued to complain and whine, I remember telling her that my best option was to just pack up my stuff and start for home the following morning.

That's when Karin said, "Before you just give up, go out there tomorrow and run their course. Show them what they will be missing out on by not interviewing you, and if it's not meant to be, then apparently that's not God's plan for us."

She was right about everything except the God part (or so I thought). At the time, I didn't pay much attention to God. Now I'm grateful that Karin was paying attention. I decided that I would take their physical exam and that I would leave a lasting impression. I had spent countless hours in the previous months preparing. Their obstacle course was right in my wheelhouse. The average elevation in Montana is 3,400 feet, which is much higher than our home state of Arkansas, so I trained even harder, knowing I would be at a disadvantage.

The next day as I sat on the grass outside the training facility, tons of thoughts were going through my head. *What if everyone else passes and I don't make an impression? Then I will have wasted even more time. What if I don't do well on the physical part or am not as prepared as I think?* All these negatives thoughts were racing through my mind as the first two applicants ran the course. The look on their faces showed that this course was very difficult, and even though it was grueling, the first few guys passed. I thought for sure I was going home. Then the next applicant failed by not finishing the course. One by one, several more applicants failed. By now, the Montana temperatures had soared into the nineties, and everyone except the Arkansas redneck was fearing the heat! The heat was normal for me. When I had left Arkansas, the temperature was more than 100 degrees with 90 percent humidity. On this Montana day, the weather for me was a bit of a relief.

We were roughly halfway through the testing when at least ten of the applicants had failed. A new hope was surging inside me, and when they called my name, I was ready. It was my turn to do what I had been working toward for months. Honestly, the course was somewhat of a blur—except the portion where you drive a steel beam six feet with a 15-pound sledgehammer. I recall hitting it and it barely moving. Then hitting it again and getting the same result. I told myself to "suck it up" and grind through. I began to strike the beam faster and harder. All the anger and frustration I had felt the day before was now being used as fuel to push me forward—and I was flying.

At the end of the day, I had not only passed the test but also beaten every other competitor except one by more than a minute, and both of us had set new course records. None of my frustration mattered anymore. I had done exactly what Karin had told me I needed to do. I had gone out there and given it my everything, and by the end of the day, I was scheduled for an interview. Only 19 people had passed, and I was at the top of the list. After the interview process, I was ranked number one on the department list, and a few short months later, Karin and I found ourselves moving across the country so I could start my new job in Montana.

Karin gets the credit. If she hadn't challenged me to "hunt the wind" by positioning myself to go after that job on the fire department, who knows what might have happened or if there would even be a *Raised Hunting* show. It was her faith in God and her belief in me that won the day. As sure as the wind is an absolute in hunting, make sure that your belief system in yourself is even more ingrained. Even when you believe in God, you must believe in yourself. Remember, the same winds that can blow you forward can also blow you off course.

THE BLACK BEDSHEET TRICK

"Hey, is that a cow?"

What if I told you that one of the best hunting tips I know is to go buy a black bedsheet? I bet that would leave you scratching your head and wondering if I had fallen out of a tree stand onto mine! I'm about to give you one of the best tools I know when it comes to hunting elk, mule deer, antelope, whitetail, and even turkeys. How many times have you spotted the animal you're after, only to discover that between you and that animal there is no cover to hide in? When the terrain makes a successful stalk unlikely, most of the time your only option is to make a huge loop, hoping to approach your prey from a better angle. In my experience, this isn't all that productive because by the time I circle back to where the animal should be, it's already gone.

Several years ago, I was glassing one of our favorite spots to hunt elk in Montana. The good Lord was smiling on us that day as we watched a large herd of elk heading toward a drainage ditch directly in front of us. About the time the elk reached the dark timber, I noticed several black beef cows not too far from the herd. There was also a really nice bull elk bedded just above them. It seemed odd to me that this bull elk was much closer to the black beef cows than he was his own herd.

What happened next forever changed the way I pack my backpack. Once the herd had disappeared into the ditch, the big bull remained bedded down even though the black cows were walking very close to him. One of the cows even walked to within ten yards of the big bull, but he was unfazed by the bovine intruder.

That's when it hit me! If we had a black sheet, two of us could walk together and look like a cow! Now, don't get me wrong— I don't believe we could have walked to within shooting range of the bull, but we could have walked across the open country to a better position.

One week later, I had a black sheet in my backpack and had an opportunity to test my theory. That day, we had 300 yards of open country between us and a small herd—a bedded bull and five cows. The two guys with me thought I was nuts when I pulled a black sheet out of my pack and said, "We're going to walk right in front of him, keeping the wind in our favor, until we get to the timber behind him." The plan worked flawlessly, and I shot that bull at 35 yards.

Since that time, we have implemented the black sheet trick on multiple species in many different states. We have sneaked across openings toward deer, turkeys, and even to within 40 yards of an antelope.

When purchasing your bedsheet look for something heavy. You don't want to be able to see through it, and you want it to last for several hunts. You can even cut holes for your head and arms. When I do this, I always wear a black facemask to ensure I can see where I'm walking.

So the next time you're doing some "spot and stalk," keep a black sheet in your pack and don't be afraid to walk right in front of the animal. I know it sounds crazy, but I promise it works.

Just don't take the sheet off your bed, because your wife will probably notice.

DAVID'S FAITH TIP

Bracing Against the Winds of Adversity

Life is full of challenges. I've learned that the only way to conquer those challenges is with God's help. I not only believe in Him; I trust Him. Complete trust in God hasn't always been easy for me, and I'll confess that sometimes it is still a bit of a stretch. You may wonder how I can call myself a Christian and in the same breath admit that there are days when it's hard for me to fully rely on God for answers. The truth is, I don't live my life trying to fool anyone or pretending to be something I am not.

It's okay to trust God and yet still have questions or even doubts when the winds of adversity are against you. I believe that God understands and knows you better than anyone else. He is fully aware of your struggles. You can't keep your struggles and pain from Him. You can hide from the animals you hunt, but you can't hide from God.

Slowly, I'm realizing that God already knows how I'm feeling whether I tell Him or not. If I keep my pain and struggle all locked up inside myself, I could easily become toxic. I am not letting God down when I'm just being honest about my lack of understanding. Rather, I'm inviting Him in so He can lift me above the storm and the winds that are against me. I really believe that my life is a lot like yours. I'm trying hard to be a good Christian. I want to do my best for God, my wife, and our boys. I want to be a good and ethical hunter. I'm guessing you too have many of those same aspirations. You and I are in this together, and God is in it with us!

When the winds of adversity are trying to blow you off course, you can be confident that God can handle the hard stuff. Just like the wind can tip off your quarry that you are in the area, the winds of adversity tell God that you need His help. Like the animals you hunt, God can also smell trouble. If you need His help, all you need to do is ask.

> *In my distress I called to the LORD;*
> *I cried to my God for help.*
> *From his temple he heard my voice;*
> *my cry came before him, into his ears.*
> **PSALM 18:6**

"It's okay to trust God and still have questions." —David Holder

ENCOURAGEMENT FROM KARIN

Well-Laid Plans

> *"For my thoughts are not your thoughts,*
> *neither are your ways my ways,"*
> *declares the LORD.*
> *"As the heavens are higher than the earth,*
> *so are my ways higher than your ways*
> *and my thoughts than your thoughts."*
> **ISAIAH 55:8-9**

In my opinion, owning and producing a national television show that is based on the behavior of wild animals is one of the most unpredictable career paths anyone could follow. The animals we hunt aren't very good at following the script. However, I believe that's what makes the show exciting. Like our audience, we never really know what is about to happen until the story unfolds. Sometimes the hunt works out exactly as we had planned, and sometimes it doesn't work out at all. At *Raised Hunting*, we have always focused on the experience and what hunting means rather than on the actual harvesting of the animal. I think that is why people can so easily relate to our family. We win some, we lose some, and we learn some.

I will throw in that even though we are not in the business of just trying to kill something, we do count on the meat from the animals we hunt as our main meat source. In 27 years of marriage, David and I have never bought beef. We prefer the clean, organic, hormone-free nutrition that wild game provides. Also, our advertisers pay for their products to be seen on a show that demonstrates a high level of success, so there is some added pressure every time we lace up our boots and grab our bows.

From the very first episode of *Raised Hunting*, David and I have always wanted our viewers to feel like they were on the hunt with us. We realize that for various reasons, watching outdoor television is the only way some people can experience the thrill of hunting. So if we can help them feel the hunt, smell the forest, or hear what we are hearing on one of our hunting adventures, we have accomplished our goal. Therefore, we do our best to share that experience in a high-quality, emotionally charged way. Not to mention the spiritual aspect of enjoying the outdoors. I know for me, getting out in nature is one of the ways I feel connected to God, as I am in awe of His fabulous creation.

Gathering the content necessary to tell a good hunting story is often difficult and sometimes leaves us wondering if the stars are ever going to align. But in my view, God is partnering with us in this venture. After all, the animals we are hunting belong to Him. It's His rain that occasionally blocks our path. It's His wind that shifts in the wrong direction while we are sitting in a favorite tree stand. These things may cause us to shake our heads in dismay, but we also know that the added difficulty makes our success that much sweeter. Hunting teaches us patience and perseverance—both of which help us succeed in other areas of our lives.

Year-round, we spend an enormous amount of time planning our hunts. We strategically place tree stands where we know the deer are using the trails nearby. We plant food plots in those same areas to help keep the deer interested in hanging around. We cut shooting lanes. We hunt the wind and use cover scents. We wear camouflage, and thanks to our industry partners, we use the best equipment available. But when God's plan is different from ours, none of that preparation matters!

When things aren't going as planned on the hunt or in life, we tend to get frustrated. We worry and maybe even get a little angry. Often, we don't stop to consider God or what He is doing. Instead of taking a step back to consider why the barrier is there in the first place, we often force the issue by trying to move forward in our own efforts. I can only speak for myself when I say that it's sometimes hard to see the big picture. I'm such a tiny piece of His creation and only a speck in time, and yet I sometimes get hung up on the things that I believe aren't going right. I can assure you that anytime I've tried to take matters into my own hands, it has always ended in complete failure.

I imagine that's how the disciples felt the night Jesus instructed them to sail their boat across the Sea of Galilee. The trip was His idea, so they must have believed that the storm that dropped seemingly out of nowhere was a mistake. And to make matters worse, Jesus was asleep in the bottom of the boat! Like David and me, at least four of the disciples worked outdoors—they were fishermen before they left their nets to follow Jesus. As a result, I'm sure they were familiar with what to do when a storm blows in. But this storm was different, and they were afraid for their lives.

> *The disciples went and woke him, saying,*
> *"Lord save us! We're going to drown!"*
> **MATTHEW 8:25**

How could this storm be a part of God's plan? Would they really go down with Jesus on board? I believe the storm wasn't a menace, but a message. A message that said, "We better go wake up Jesus." When you have an interruption in your life, you have the same opportunity. Jesus didn't allow His disciples to drown, and He won't leave you in the crashing waves either.

> *Then he got up and rebuked*
> *the winds and the waves,*
> *and it was completely calm.*
> **MATTHEW 8:26**

REFLECTION

When the storms of life suddenly appear out of nowhere, how will you "wake up" Jesus?

6

USE YOUR FEAR

Don't Be Afraid to Be Afraid

I remember standing on a mountain in Montana, fighting for every breath. I was in awe of the beauty surrounding me and equally scared to death. For the first time in my hunting career, I felt like I had bitten off more than I could chew. The vast expanse of mountains stretched for miles as far as I could see in every direction. Getting there wasn't easy, and to be honest, I wasn't exactly sure how I would get back.

I grew up in Virginia and later moved to Arkansas. Harsh terrain was no mystery to me. I had hunted mountains, marshes, and swamps. But none of those places had ever given me a feeling quite like I was experiencing that day. Until that moment, I had never been afraid of anything outdoors. Sure, I was cautious of snakes, poison ivy, and rugged terrain—but never afraid. The mountains of Montana were enormous, and I began to wonder if I could actually hunt there. What if they were too big for this Arkansas boy?

I knew where the fear was coming from, but I was still having trouble shutting it down and calming my mind. The fear I felt that day was rooted in the unknown. The mountain I had just climbed wasn't nearly as big as other mountains I would have to climb if I wanted to hunt in this location. It was clear to me that not too many hunters chose this location—likely because of the difficulty of the terrain—and I couldn't help but wonder how I would navigate my way in or out.

I decided to go for it even if I had to do it afraid. Just the thought of being able to hunt where others couldn't was all the drive I needed. It was time to conquer the fear that had wrapped itself around my thoughts.

Keep in mind this was long before the days of smartphones or Google Maps, so I didn't have access to exact coordinates, wind direction, or weather reports. All I had was a map of the general area and a compass—both of which I learned to use immediately after moving out west. I wasn't much on asking others for help, so I had been taking weekend hiking trips into this area—each time going back a little farther until I felt like I was ready to try this elk hunting thing. Everything I learned about the mountains, I learned the hard way.

All that preparation had paid off as I was now miles off the beaten path. Using my compass and my map, I set up camp exactly where I had planned. I knew this area was untouched by other hunters, as there were no trails or signs that others had been here. In my excitement, I almost forgot the fear that had paralyzed me just a few moments earlier. After setting up camp, there were still two hours of daylight left— just enough time to scout for the elk I had come to hunt.

The temperatures were perfect and noticeably cooler than in town. With a light breeze, the late July afternoon was comfortable. As I sat near my mini home away from home, I thought, *It really doesn't get any better than this.* The only thing left for me to do was get out my map and find the spot I had previously dubbed "Lookout." That was where I wanted to hunt.

Lookout was high on the ridge above me and faced the northern slope. It was mostly clear of trees and the kind of place a bull would go if he wanted to stay comfortable, cool, and hidden from the summer sun. I worked my way up the steep mountain without a trail or clearly defined landmarks. The terrain and trees all looked the same. I was 30 minutes from the camp when I came to an opening in the timber.

I hadn't considered the sheer size of the trees that were blocking my view of the opening I was hoping to hunt on the side of the adjoining mountain. Frustrated, I could see what appeared to be another opening just ahead of me and decided to go check it out. When I got there, it was exactly as I had hoped. I could see for miles, and there was heavy timber all around with open areas mixed in. It only improved when I saw two velvet-antlered bulls feeding on the northern slope at the edge of the dark timber.

I will never forget that moment. I had done it. I had pushed past my fears, and now I was looking at what most hunters only dream about. Just a few short hours ago, I was looking at this very spot in my binoculars and thinking about how I would never make it this far. But I had made it, I was comfortable, and I could find my way back out.

If I had allowed my fears to take over and win, I would have still been standing on the distant mountain wondering what this spot looked like. I would have missed out on one of the most beautiful sights these eyes have seen and the satisfaction of knowing that I was the kind of hunter who could get to such a place. Having been both the guy looking from a distance and the guy who closed the distance, I can tell you that I'm nothing special. I just refuse to allow fear to determine the course or quality of my life.

My hunting career has included hundreds of instances when fear could have stopped me dead in my tracks. I would be lying if I said there haven't been times where I've pushed the pause button because I was quivering in my boots. It's taken me a while, but I've concluded that being afraid isn't a failure. Never trying because of fear—that's failure. So every time fear tries to creep in, I think about that mountain in Montana. I remind myself how I would have missed out on one of the best moments of my life had I allowed fear to take the reins.

Always practice safety while spending time outdoors, but don't be afraid to be afraid. Everything you've been dreaming about is on the other side of what you're most afraid of.

DAVID'S LIFE TIP

Never Allow Fear to Stop You

Karin and I have certainly lived in some wonderful places. We moved from Virginia to Arkansas out of necessity—I wanted to make a fresh start by not going down the same path of addiction as many of the other men in my family. Seeing the destruction all around me left a giant hole in my heart, and I wondered if I would be next. So our first relocation was a strategic move away from an environment that could have destroyed me. It wasn't easy to pack up and leave everything I had become accustomed to, but something was telling me I had to get out of there.

Our move to Montana was something we chose to do to better our lives. This time, I wasn't running from anything or trying to escape possible destruction. I was searching for something more fulfilling, satisfying, and challenging. In Arkansas, Karin and I had learned how to live on our own. Every young couple goes through that phase of trying to figure out how to make it without Mom and Dad. We struggled at first but quickly adapted. Karin had a successful job as a nail technician, and I had a promising career as a fireman, but something was missing. The fire department that I worked for ran very few calls, and our 24-hour shifts usually consisted of sitting on the couch, sleeping, watching television, or rescuing the occasional cat stuck in a tree. I wanted more, and so did Karin. So she began looking for our next challenge.

Within a few months, we were notified that I had been offered a position with a much larger fire department in Montana. This job was the career opportunity I had been looking for. The department was three times larger and ran ten times as many calls. There was also the chance for advancement. But there were two issues: First, it was 1,700 miles from where we lived in Arkansas. Second, Warren was only six weeks old at the time. It was mid-February, and they wanted us there in two weeks. Looking back, I guess we should have asked for more time to pack and get our lives in order. Instead, we happily complied.

After I accepted the offer, I hung up the phone and looked at Karin.

I could tell that she felt exactly as I did. Neither of us knew whether to be happy or terrified.

It was time to pack, make the dreaded call to our parents, and move to the middle of nowhere. That's normal, right? Not hardly! My parents were afraid for us and offered to come help move our things. I tried to tell them no, but as good parents, they could tell we really needed a hand, especially with Warren.

One week later, we were on the road to Montana. Our small caravan consisted of my parents' car, my truck, and a moving van pulling Karin's car. Everything we owned was once again en route to a new location, only this time, the unknowns were piled high, as Karin and I wouldn't have a single family member within 1,700 miles. There would be no way to reach out to Grandpa or Grandma should the need arise.

The trip started well, and the weather was very nice. Everything was fine until we reached Wyoming. I don't know if it was Karin seeing tumbleweeds for the first time or the antelope wandering around in the yard of the Motel 6 where we stayed that night, but for the first time, I saw fear in her eyes. The farther we drove, the colder it got and the more nervous she became. I began to worry about her.

Fear has a way of causing you to forget the facts. Karin and I were struggling to keep it together. I wanted to tell her that it was okay because we were doing the right thing and that we weren't all going to die of frostbite. But the words never came as we drove through what seemed like a never-ending frozen plain and our anxiety continued to build. When we arrived in Great Falls, the temperature dropped to ten below zero, and the Realtor I had been in contact with was no longer in the area.

Now we were beyond nervous and beginning to question our decision to move so far away from our home in Arkansas. Everyone was stressed out. We had no solid plan, just a job. We had a lot to do and no place to live. This would have been a good time for Karin or me to have a meltdown, but instead of one of us losing it, my dad lost it. I remember as he sobbed at the table of our hotel that night, questioning why in the world we would choose to move to Montana.

We were all trying to console him when Karin said, "Pop, God has brought us this far. I'm sure He isn't going to leave us out in the street to freeze to death. Everything is going to work out. You'll see." For whatever reason, her words sounded funny to all of us. So instead of crying and whining, we began laughing uncontrollably, picturing all of us out in the street freezing to death while people just drove by without even noticing.

Back then I would have told you it was a coincidence that our move to Montana somehow worked out. But today I can tell you Karin was right. God was taking care of us all along. The next day, a firefighter I hadn't met yet called and said he had heard we were having trouble finding a place to live. He explained that he had an ex-girlfriend with a house for rent right there in town, and if we could meet her within a few minutes, she could show it to us and we could move in immediately.

In an instant, all our worries and fears melted away. We were no longer worried about the move. We had mustered up every ounce of courage we could find (which was a little more than my dad could muster). We had faced our fears by refusing to focus on what could go wrong. Had Karin and I allowed fear to stop us, we wouldn't be where we are today. We wouldn't be *who* we are today.

Fear is relentless and will always be there to tell you what you can and cannot do. Our family's greatest accomplishments have always been on the other side of fear. If you're going to be afraid, be afraid of the life you could miss out on because of fear. Karin and I believe in you. God believes in you. Decide to believe in yourself.

HUNT THE CLUSTER

*The perfect tree to hang your
stand from is actually a group of trees.*

While preseason scouting for whitetails, it's important to pay attention to the game trails. You can learn a lot from the paths that take the most pounding. But once you've identified where you want to hunt, it's not always easy to find the right tree to hang a stand in.

I believe the wind direction is the most important element to consider when choosing a tree stand location, but I also believe that how you conceal yourself in the tree stand is critical. My family and I always try to choose the best camo pattern we can find to match our surroundings, and we never set our stands where we will be silhouetted by an approaching deer. And in my 40-plus years of chasing the wily whitetail across several states, I have found another little nugget to share with you.

Hunt the cluster. If given the choice between a lone tree 15 yards from the trail and a cluster of trees 23 yards from the trail, choose the cluster every time. A cluster of trees will help break up your outline and protect you from being spotted in the tree. I hunt in all sorts of clusters, but my favorite is to find a cluster that allows me to hunt with a few of the trees in front of me. This provides plenty of cover, and I can always find several holes to shoot through.

Vines or heavy foliage, such as berries and ivy, also make great clusters. We have used one of our tree stands for eight years, and it has become so thick with foliage on one side of the tree, we can hunt a mere eight feet off the ground. That stand is where we are most concealed and least likely to be spotted by a deer.

If you can't find a cluster of trees or a tree with heavy foliage, try to find a tree with large limbs. All you're really looking for is something to provide additional cover. The next time you're looking to place a deer stand, always take into consideration how well you will be hidden.

Remember, deer are used to seeing that tree, and you don't want them to notice any big differences when you're in it, or they will adjust their travel patterns accordingly. Don't just bank on height or wind direction. Keep in mind that as important as those are, so is concealment. Staying hidden will ensure that you can hunt that stand year after year. If you start getting spotted in that tree, the deer will probably move to another trail.

If you find the cluster, the deer won't find you.

DAVID'S FAITH TIP

"Courage Is Fear That Has Said Its Prayers"

What are you afraid of, and how do you handle that fear? I'm guessing it's not hard to come up with a short list of your fears. The difficult part is handling them. It's easy to tell ourselves not to be afraid, but rarely do we know how to stop being afraid.

I'm a bit OCD, which means I am strong-willed, and for a good portion of my life, I was afraid to give God full control. Sure, I would allow Him to help when I really needed it and felt like I couldn't do something on my own. I would even complain when He didn't help me the way I expected Him to. I'm not proud of that behavior, and I have to remind myself daily that my job as a follower of Christ is to follow His lead by refusing to follow my own.

I've learned that my walk with God is very similar to the mountain in Montana that left me gasping for air that day. Nothing says you have to learn how to follow God overnight. In fact, you can't. Just as I had to practice hiking in and back out before tackling a full-blown elk hunt, I have to practice and build endurance as I learn to follow Jesus.

Sometimes I ask God to help me stop struggling or doubting His plan for my life. I wish I could tell you that He suddenly shows up in a bright light and wipes away all my fear. It doesn't happen that way, but I'm learning to watch as He works. We will never forget hearing Karin say "God hasn't brought us this far to just leave us" and the next day finding a place to live. That experience will always remind us why we don't have to fear. When we can't figure out what to do but suddenly a perfect solution comes together, we sense that we are not alone.

I think a good question might be, If we know God has our best interest in mind, why do we fear turning our lives over to Him? I can't answer for you, but I can tell you why I think I sometimes struggle with this concept. Perhaps you can relate. In my mind, if I give God my whole life, then I no longer have total control. I might have to do some things I don't want to do. If I give Him my life, I'm surrendering my future to someone who occasionally does something I don't understand. Sometimes I feel as if I know what is best—even when God is offering a different path.

I have been quick to forget that all Jesus really wants from me is to trust in His plan and to faithfully follow the path He carves out. In the Gospels, the disciples often didn't understand what Jesus was doing or saying but had to trust Him anyway. Honestly, I'm the guy who still asks God to explain the details to me—or better yet, show them to me. If only He would make the picture clear, believing would be easier for me. Then I remember that God isn't asking me to believe in a clearly drawn picture; He is asking me to have faith when the picture looks more like scattered puzzle pieces. I've always believed in God, but it wasn't until later in my life that I learned to have faith in His plan.

We have a choice: We can live in fear (like I did for so many years), or we can live in faith (like I'm trying my best to do now). Each of us must make that choice every day.

Jesus replied, "You do not realize now what I am doing,
but later you will understand."

JOHN 13:7

―――――――― **ENCOURAGEMENT FROM KARIN** ――――――――

Be Still

"Be still," David said. "There's a bull elk staring right at us. He has us pinned!"

"No way," I whispered, trying not to move a single muscle.

"I'm not kidding, Karin. He's staring right at us."

Just an hour earlier, David, Warren, our cameraman Josh, and I had worked our way around a steep mountainside. This would be our last setup on this hunt as we were literally out of time. We had been hunting hard for three days, and David's elk tag was still in his pocket. We knew going in that three days isn't much time for an elk hunt, but our hunting schedule was tight that fall, so we had no other option. We could either roll the dice and hunt for three days or not hunt at all. We chose to roll the dice.

On this hunt, we had several encouraging encounters, but we were never able to seal the deal. After three days of giving it all we had, we decided to try one last time. This would be our final attempt at one of the bull elk we knew were in the area. We found an open field, and the wind was perfect. Warren was doing the calling and had set up about 50 yards behind us. I was filming, and David was the shooter. Josh was tucked under a cedar bush, filming from a different angle.

Warren bugled and then made a series of cow calls. He was trying to gain the attention of a dominant bull we hoped would come in looking for a fight. Warren called and called, but to no avail. After 30 minutes or so, Warren stopped calling and came up to join the rest of us. We all just sat, completely defeated. Our bodies were sore from all the hiking and carrying heavy gear through the mountains, and our minds were tired from all the near misses. We had done everything we knew to do, but the hunt was over. I asked David to do a closing interview for our show, and even though the air around us was thick with disappointment, he agreed. Once the interview was over, I reached up and turned off the camera. It was time to go home.

That's when it happened. David said, "Be still—there's a bull elk staring right at us. He has us pinned!" David was facing the opposite direction of the bull, and his bow was lying by his side. He was completely unprepared. I was behind him, just kind of bent over in an awkward position, but I somehow found a way to get the camera back on. The bull was intently giving us the once-over and trying hard to figure out exactly what we were. From the corner of my eye, I could see David moving extremely slow as if he was going to get a shot at this bull. But he would have to get his release back on, nock an arrow, and somehow get turned around. I was doing my best to focus the camera, terrified that this bull would catch the slightest movement and be gone forever.

Thirteen minutes later, we were all still in the same position—including the bull. My legs were starting to cramp and tremble. I prayed, *God, please help me be still. I don't want to be the one to blow this hunt.* David's breathing picked up—faster and deeper. I knew he was about to do something drastic. Ever so slowly, he raised his bow and twisted. In one smooth movement, he was able to draw his bow and get positioned for a shot. David's arrow perfectly hit its mark!

The bull turned and ran, crashing through the timber as he went. I fell over and gave a sigh of relief. Warren jumped up and said, "Did that really just happen?" David was shaking and speechless. He had just made the most incredible shot I have ever heard of, let alone witnessed! The difficulty of what he had just done cannot be adequately described. Josh soon joined us for a group hug.

One minute we were in a pit of disappointment, but only 13 minutes later we were overcome with joy. There was no real reason that bull didn't see us other than we were still. I'm convinced that God's hand was in the entire situation and that he was teaching the *Raised Hunting* family a lesson on the importance of stillness.

When you do not stop to be still, you cannot clearly hear what God is trying to say to you. When your own thoughts are dominating your thinking or your mind is engaged in constant interaction with others, it is nearly impossible to hear from God. On this hunt, God waited until we got still. Once we were still, God put His plan into action and our hunt ended in smiles.

Be still, and know that I am God.

PSALM 46:10

Sometimes when you think it's over, it's not really over. This bull was taken 15 minutes after the closing interview that ended our 2015 Montana elk hunt!

REFLECTION

When was the last time you were still before God? What did He say to you? How will you practice being still in the future?

7

DON'T PUSH

Leave and Come Back

Every pro tip written in this book is very important. Each has the power to determine your success as an ultimate hunter. Overlooking the tip I'm about to share with you could end in catastrophe for the animal. As I've stated many times at *Raised Hunting*, we believe that we owe it to the animals we hunt to harvest them as humanely as possible. However, even those of us with the best intentions can unintentionally wound an animal.

As much as I would love to say I can help you track down every wounded animal, I can't. There are, however, some techniques that can help, such as finding blood or figuring out where an animal might go after it's wounded. I've heard it said that a wounded animal will go to water and usually travel downhill, but in my experience, that is not always the case. I've discovered that every species of animal has its own unique way of dealing with an injury. An elk, for example, will walk for miles when injured, while a whitetail deer will often look for cover. A turkey will dig into the brush to hide, but an antelope will put some distance between itself and the perceived danger before bedding down.

Those are some quick tips that have helped me over the years, but let's get specific and talk about what to do when you know your shot placement was off and the animal is no longer in the area.

As with most of the tips in this book, I had to learn the hard way how to track and find a wounded animal. One specific elk hunt comes to mind. On this hunt, everything was going right, and I was finally beginning to believe that I had what it took to be an elk hunter. I was hunting a big meadow on public ground where elk gathered to feed every morning. When I got to my hidden meadow, I stopped and glassed, and I could see at least 200 elk in the predawn light. The only problem that I had was the wind. If I tried to move in now, it would blow my scent straight in the direction of the herd. I knew that circling around to the other side of the meadow in the dark wasn't a good idea because the terrain was thick and rugged. I only had one option. I would have to wait at a distance for the elk to leave and for the morning thermals to change. Then I could approach the elk by creeping up a dry creek bed, keeping cover between me and the elk. I would have the wind in my face as I made my approach.

Do you have any idea how hard it is to watch that many elk without going after them? I do! But my patience paid off, and eventually they broke up into smaller groups of about 50 and started back up the mountain. About 9:30 a.m., my prayers were answered as the wind began to shift. It was no longer blowing on my back and was now blowing straight in my face. All I had to do now was get above the elk and slip down to one of the herds.

As I got in position, everything was coming together perfectly. I was above the herd, and I could hear them bugling and moving around just below me. My plan was to make a few soft cow calls and lure one of the big bulls away from the herd. I did not expect what happened next.

After making one or two soft calls, I looked to my left and saw a nice six-by-seven bull standing less than 20 yards away. To my surprise, he walked past me at five yards, but I was sitting on the ground and was in no position to turn around for a good shot. I had one chance at that bull. There was a big tree just ahead of him, so I made up my mind that would be my opportunity to draw my bow.

Once the bull's head was behind the tree, I came to full draw. Just as the bull cleared the tree, I released my arrow. The bull made an unexpected slight turn toward me. The arrow hit right behind his shoulder but came out on the other side in the middle of his body. That shot wasn't good, and I knew it immediately. As he was running off, he was also spooking all the other elk in the area and causing them to run. In the chaos of what was happening, I lost track of the elk I had just shot.

I panicked and frantically began to try to locate him. Finally, after the woods calmed down, I could see antlers. There was a bull standing in the timber below me. I got out my binoculars. By the hole in his side, I knew he was my elk. It was now 11:00 a.m. I sat down and prayed that he would tip over and that would be it. An hour went by—then another—and I still watched that elk. Several more hours went by. As the sun began to set and darkness was rolling in, I had a decision to make. Did I dare leave the elk overnight and return the next morning, or should I try to slip close enough to get another shot? As I mentioned earlier, elk usually walk when they are injured, and since the bull wasn't walking, I knew it was just a matter of time until the bull expired.

In my opinion, the decision to either leave or finish off an animal is one of the hardest a bowhunter can make. Nobody likes to leave a wounded animal, and your heart is pulling at you to go do the humane thing by ending the animal's suffering. After weighing my options, I decided that "bumping" this bull was not a risk I was willing to take.

My decision to leave wasn't a quick or easy one. It was a decision born out of hours of anguish. The walk back to my truck was five miles, and if I wanted to make it before midnight, I had to leave immediately. With every step, I couldn't believe that I was actually leaving the giant elk with no guarantees that he would even be there in the morning. If you've ever been in a similar situation, you know how sleepless those nights can be when you're waiting to see if you made the right choice by returning the next day. After all, you've worked so hard to get to that moment only to have something go terribly wrong.

After a night of trying to figure out how I could have handled the situation differently, morning finally came. I decided to pack everything I would need to bring an elk out of the timber. I had no way of knowing whether the bull would still be there, but I wanted to be prepared just in case. The entire time I was walking, I was also praying. *Please, God. Let me find him.*

Once I was close to where the elk should be, I laid down all my gear and then continued until I made it to the spot where I had stood and watched him for hours the day before. I glassed and glassed but found no sign of him. I started down the hill to see what I could find. With every step, I felt both hope and anguish. At first, I saw nothing. I began to question my decision to leave. I thought, *What if I don't find this bull?*

I took a few more steps and instantly felt relief as I saw an antler. There he was, lying on his side. It looked as if he had worked the arrow out sometime during the night. At that moment, I knew that if I had pushed that elk, if I had gone down there right after I had shot him, this story would have had a much different ending. I would be telling you the story of an elk I lost because I refused to leave and come back.

The decision to leave an animal you have shot is never easy. But "when in doubt, back out." On this hunt, following that rule made for a sleepless night, but thankfully, it led to an easy recovery the next morning.

You cannot push a wounded animal. I have read books that say to wait six hours on a gut-shot animal, but I have personally seen animals live as long as eighteen hours after a bad shot. It's an agonizing decision not to go look for an animal, especially when bad weather or night-fall is approaching. But it's even tougher to lose an animal because you didn't wait. It's one thing when an animal is hurt, but it's something completely different when an animal is hurt and knows a human is in the area. If you push them, you may never find them.

———————— DAVID'S LIFE TIP ————————

Don't Push Your Kids—Pull Them

It's one thing to push a wounded animal, but what about the stuff that matters most—like pushing the people you love? I truly believe that pushing someone when they aren't ready isn't the same as pulling the best out of them.

For example, let's say it's the fourth quarter of a football game. You're down by six points with a minute left on the clock, and you're on the 50-yard line. Anyone who knows me will tell you that if I'm your coach, I'm going to be pulling the best out of you by insisting that you fight for every yard gained as you do your best to score the winning touchdown.

It's extremely tough as a parent to know when you've crossed the line between pushing your kids and pulling the best out of them. I've seen this with our boys, Warren and Easton. By the time Warren was three years old, I knew that he was going to be obsessed with hunting. Warren was always pretending to hunt. He never went anywhere as a kid without a bow or a call of some sort in his hand. However, it wasn't like that with Easton. Don't get me wrong—Easton loves to hunt, but he has always been the athlete in our family. Unlike Warren, Easton enjoys other interests more than hunting.

Honestly, there have been times when I've pushed Easton to pursue his athletic abilities. I've even explained to him that God doesn't just give that kind of talent to everybody and that he should take advantage of the blessings God has given him. But baseball season collides with turkey season, and football season goes well into bow season, so Easton felt pulled in both directions.

I love to hunt with my boys and can remember the days when all three of us would climb into a ladder stand. One of my greatest memories while hunting is of shooting a doe with all three of us in the tree together. (Before you bust me for not being safe, let me assure you that all three of us were wearing safety harnesses.) My only regret is that we couldn't fit Karin in the tree with us! I remember laughing and giggling as they did the goofiest stuff. I will never know how we managed to kill that deer.

The day came when Easton began to show a lack of interest in hunting, deciding that he would rather play sports or go to a friend's house than spend time in the woods. For me, hearing those words felt like a punch in the stomach because hunting has always been something our family lives for and can do together. I now had one son who still loved to go hunting and another son who wanted to do other things with his time.

This created a real problem for me, since I couldn't be in two places at once. How could I be in the woods with Warren and at a ball game watching Easton? So I handled it the only way I knew how. I split my time between them and didn't try to push Easton into hunting simply because it was something we had always done in the past. Just like with the elk, I knew better than to push.

If I had forced Easton to go on our hunting trips when he didn't want to go, he could have easily grown to dislike hunting. As I write this chapter, I can tell you that Easton still loves to hunt; he just doesn't have the same passion for hunting that Warren does, and that's okay. I wish I could tell you that it was easy for me to learn how to let Easton be his own person, but I can't.

I had to take a step back and allow my youngest son to decide what mattered most to him. If hunting wasn't on the top of his list, then I had no right to tell him otherwise. He had to be allowed to find his own way without me pushing him. I'm proud of him for standing up to me and telling me that he didn't want to hunt at the same pace as the rest of his family. It's taken me a while, but I'm no longer on Easton's case about hunting more. I do, however, try to pull the best out of him in other areas, reminding him to be on time and to always leave a place better than he found it.

Now that Easton is grown and moved out on his own, I still try to communicate with him by listening as he explains his new passions. I've stopped focusing on what I want for his life and started trusting that he knows what will put fuel in his tank. I now know when to back off and when to step in. Wherever Easton goes or whatever he does, he will be more than fine, even if he never steps foot in another tree stand.

Pulling your kids in the direction of their dreams works better than pushing them in the direction of yours.

THE BEST GAME CALLS ARE FREE

Just do what you've heard.

One day, a big buck ran past my tree stand several times. He was grunting every step of the way and never considered slowing down long enough for me to get a shot. When he and the doe with him finally headed into a tiny quarter-acre thicket right in the middle of the two bean fields I was hunting, I knew I had to make my move.

I climbed down out of my stand and sneaked over to the edge of the thicket. I knew that if I made a few grunts on my grunt call, the buck would likely come running. I grunted at him once, but the big deer was a no-show. So I grunted again and then a third time, but still, he was nowhere to be seen. I was positive the buck was still in the thicket, but I couldn't figure out why he wasn't responding to my calls. Then I remembered that when he had run by me, he was stiff-legged, pounding his feet on the ground with each step.

Nearby, a farmer had piled some rocks from his field, and

that gave me an idea. The next time I grunted, I pounded two rocks on the ground, simulating the hooves of another buck chasing a doe. Immediately, I looked to my left and saw the big buck staring at me from only 15 yards away! I never killed that deer—in fact, I didn't even have time to get my bow in my hands before he was gone. But what I did get that day was a tactic that would eventually bring me future success.

I love to use game calls, but what I love more is the feeling that I truly understand the animals I hunt and that I'm effectively communicating with them. So when I started implementing realism—a cow elk breaking sticks as she walks through the woods or the sound of her walking across shale rocks—my communication with the animals I was pursuing became much more effective. A lot of people use game calls, but very few use them while slapping a limb on the water of a wallow to simulate an elk thrashing around in the mud.

The best calls in the world can only communicate so much. By adding a touch of realism, you are more likely to be successful, especially when an animal is heavily pressured. Raking the leaves with your antlers or pounding them on the ground as you clash them together may be exactly what you need for a buck that has been around the block a few times. As much as I would love to tell you that the best game calls are made by a certain company, that's not the case. The best game calls are often free and are waiting for you to implement them at the right time and in the right way. It cost me nothing that day to smash two rocks on the ground when my buck was buried in the thicket.

The next time you're thinking about adding a call to your hunt, consider exactly what you've heard the animal you're after do in the past. What sounds have you heard, and how can you replicate those sounds? Once you learn to replicate what you've heard in the woods, you will have more encounters with the animals you love to chase.

DAVID'S FAITH TIP

Lead Them to Jesus, Don't Push Them

I consider myself an average person. My life probably looks a lot like yours. Sure, my family has a national television show, but I also face the same challenges that you do. Being on TV doesn't remove me from everyday life. As I write this, I'm doing my best to be honest and share with you not only my success but also my failure. As we've discussed in this chapter, when you push an animal or a person—you could end up losing them forever. The pressure you put on them could become the door they walk through as they exit your life.

In the same way, I believe that people of strong faith can be too pushy when it comes to sharing their faith. Don't get me wrong—as a believer myself, I know that we are called not only to live out our faith in Jesus but to share it as well. My concern is that, just like in hunting, sometimes you can push too hard. Even with the best of intentions, we can push people further from the cross instead of drawing them closer.

You can't push people to the cross, but you can lead them there.

I've dealt with my fair share of well-meaning believers who accidentally do more harm than good. For example, they may proclaim that when people follow Jesus, all the bad things in their lives go away and they don't have nearly as many problems. These would-be evangelists treat Jesus almost like a genie in a bottle or a pill that instantly fixes every problem, rather than a loving Savior who wants to have a relationship with them. When someone is wounded and in a dark place, they don't necessarily need to be pushed into seeking an answer. They need to be gently led to Jesus, who is the Answer. We can lead people to Jesus simply by being good examples.

For years, I didn't go to church, and I was never taught why I needed to have a solid relationship with God. To be honest, I just didn't think about it. So when someone said to me that I needed to have more of God in my life, I didn't necessarily disagree with them—it just wasn't on my radar. I can tell you that no amount of pushing would have reached David Holder. It wasn't until Karin and I went through some hard problems in our marriage that I realized I needed something bigger than me to lean on. Just like I couldn't push Easton to love hunting, no one could push me to love Jesus. Rather, Karin's quiet faith and the example she set for our marriage brought me to Christ.

At *Raised Hunting*, I don't think that we are overly religious or that we push Jesus down our viewers' throats. Yet I get tons of messages from those who watch our shows saying how much they love the fact that the Holders are a family of strong faith. Even though Karin and I don't consider ourselves preachers, people often see Jesus in our lives just by watching the show.

We once submitted the very first episode of *Raised Hunting* to another network for consideration. They said that we had great content (other than the Christian stuff that would need to be edited out) and that they would like us to join their network. I honestly had no idea what they were talking about when they said we were "too Christian." I had to go back and watch my own pilot episode to see what the fuss was all about.

As it turned out, they were referring to Karin sitting on the couch and flipping through her Bible. That scene wasn't staged as part of the episode; it was just Karin doing what she normally does. They also noticed the cross hanging around my neck. I didn't wear that cross for the show; I always wear a cross. In both instances, Karin and I weren't being overtly Christian—we were just being who we are. In the end, we decided not to partner with that network because they were asking us to change who we are.

I am thankful for the people in my life who drip Jesus on me instead of pouring Him over me like a bucket of ice water. And that's what we try to do at *Raised Hunting*. We don't want to push so hard we push people away, and we don't believe God wants us to do that either. Lead them to Jesus, don't push them.

In the same way, let your light shine before others, that they may see your good deeds and glorify your Father in heaven.
MATTHEW 5:16

ENCOURAGEMENT FROM KARIN

The Unlikely Candidate

When I first started bowhunting with David, I noticed that very few women were enjoying the sport. I think a lot of ladies grew up around hunting but never really had the opportunity to pick up a bow and arrow. Times are changing as more women are either hunting or shooting archery.

As I began to enjoy bowhunting, I often felt like I didn't belong or wasn't a good fit. It didn't help matters that I was often the only woman in every hunting camp or event that David and I attended. If I wanted to continue shooting my bow, I had to push aside those negative thoughts of feeling out of place and go on in confidence. Spending time with David, Warren, and Easton while shooting bows is still one of my favorite ways to spend the day. Back then, I was an unlikely candidate. Now I'm just the girl who outshoots most of the boys.

David has always supported my love for bowhunting and goes out of his way to make sure I get ample time in the woods when bow season rolls around. One of the things I love the most is seeing my husband at his best. David is a great man, but when he is hunting, his level of greatness increases as he is doing what God has called him to do. God has gifted him with the ability to understand the behavior of animals in a way that seems unnatural. I would call it supernatural.

David and I are doing our best to follow God's plan not only in the woods together but also in our daily lives. I can't speak for David, but I know that I don't always feel qualified to do what God is requiring of me. When it comes to following God's lead, I occasionally get that same uneasy feeling that I had back when I was the only woman on the archery range.

I can relate to Moses of the Old Testament. When God said to Moses that He was sending him to Pharaoh to lead the Israelites out of slavery in Egypt, Moses questioned his ability to follow God's call. Moses felt like an unlikely candidate, even saying, "Who am I that I should go to Pharaoh?" (Exodus 3:11).

Like Moses, I have been guilty of asking God that same question. *Why are You asking me to do this? Don't You know that I'm in no way qualified? Why don't You find someone else with more ability?* Self-doubt is always trying to creep in and take over my mind. Not to mention the fact that Satan doesn't want me to accomplish any of God's purposes for my life or walk in the future God has planned for me. Satan is always reminding me of everything I believe I'm not. He whispers, "You're not only unlikely—you're the least likely." I'm learning to tune him out, and you must do the same.

You might be wondering how the story of Moses relates to women in the outdoors. As I read the story of Moses, I truly believe that a lot of his apprehension came from the fact that he had never been in that situation before. It's the unknown that usually creates doubt.

I know women who I believe would love hunting and the outdoor culture, but because they don't understand it or they feel out of place, they have a wall built up around the very idea of participating in an outdoor lifestyle. In my opinion, they are missing out on a great opportunity. Some of the best moments of my life have happened in a hunting camp or sitting around a campfire with my family and friends. Not to mention the fact that I get to know what my sons are up to when we are hanging out in a tree stand together for eight hours. I also get to see my husband using his God-given talent while we are on one of our adventures.

May I offer a little friendly advice? Don't count yourself out before giving hunting (or anything else, for that matter) your best shot. Moses came up with several reasons he wasn't the one to lead the people out of slavery. He even asked God to send someone else to do it (Exodus 4:13). Refuse to disqualify yourself. When God gets involved, the unlikely becomes the most likely.

REFLECTION

Are you allowing negative self-talk or doubts to keep you from something you know God has called you to? What will you do to move forward?

Be strong in the Lord and in his mighty power.
EPHESIANS 6:10

8

GO THE EXTRA MILE

Work to Get the Upper Hand

I believe life, marriage, parenting, hunting, and my relationship with God all deserve my best. Karin says I don't know how to give less than 110 percent. She is right—especially when I'm hunting. I'm wired to pay attention and always try to keep myself focused even when it's midday and the chances of animal movement are slim. I realize there is always a chance to harvest an animal when the conditions are less than perfect. One thing is for sure—I've never killed anything while sitting on my couch.

In life and in hunting, I strive to have the upper hand, and this requires doing the extra little bit that most people aren't willing to do. I believe that when you do more than others are willing to do, you can accomplish more than they can.

This philosophy has served me well over the years, and in my opinion, it tipped the scales in my favor on a particularly difficult whitetail deer hunt. In chapter 1, I referred to a heartbreaking missed opportunity I had with a giant whitetail. In case you've forgotten, it was my account of why you never go into the woods with a Velcro strap on your release. What I didn't tell you is that only three days later I had a second encounter with that same buck. I was hunting near where I had first seen him but in a different stand.

As I prepared for the last two days of the hunt, I explained my new strategy to my hunting partner. Two small food plots sat at the bottom of a ridge with a small road joining them. The plan was to set up a buck decoy in the middle of the road. My hope was that a shooter buck would venture into one of the food plots, see the decoy, and get curious enough to come to check it out. The only problem was, I didn't have a decoy with me on that trip. After making a few inquiries, I finally located a small, scruffy, one-horned buck decoy that looked more like a dog with leprosy than a deer! It was my only option, so I had to use it. The plan was to sit in the stand all day. The weather was changing, and the forecast was calling for heavy rains. My hunting buddy wasn't willing to fight the bad weather, but I had already made up my mind to hunt come rain or shine.

The next morning it was raining, but barely. When I got to my stand, the temperature was in the thirties and not expected to rise. After only a few minutes, a little doe strolled by, and I thought, *Oh boy, this is going to work!* I wish I could tell you that deer began to pour into the food plots, but that's not the case. Instead, the drizzle of rain turned into a downpour. I've never seen it rain so hard in my life! My decoy was only 16 yards from where I was standing, and on more than one occasion, it was raining so hard that I couldn't see the decoy.

My hunting partner had left a truck for me at the top of the hill just in case I wanted to call it quits, but I had already decided that if I wanted to kill a good buck, staying put was my only option. All I could think about was what could potentially happen if the rain would only stop for a few minutes. I knew that the deer would be moving, and I wanted to be ready if that were to happen. I stood for eight hours as three and a half inches of cold rain fell.

Near the end of the day, it finally happened—the rain stopped, and I could see some blue sky between the clouds. With only an hour of daylight left, I started to get excited. I anticipated that every deer in the country would be stirring soon. But I now had a new problem—the rain had been so heavy that it had found a path through my rain gear. The bottom half of my body was soaking wet, and I was starting to shiver. I knew I had to dig deep and push through if I wanted to have a chance of killing a deer. That was my "extra mile" moment. I could pack up my gear and head to the truck, or I could grind through the last few moments of this hunt. I wrung the water out of my gloves, put them back on, and committed to hanging around until dark.

A few minutes later, I caught movement about 300 yards away. I could tell it was a big deer, but my binoculars were so fogged up from all the rain that I couldn't use them. I grabbed my rattling antlers and smashed them together as hard as I could. I did it again and again before hanging them back up. From that distance, I couldn't tell whether the buck heard me, and I could no longer see him.

After about 15 minutes, I decided to try the rattling antlers one more time. But before I could do that, the buck appeared in the food plot in front of me. I still vividly remember how wide and heavy his rack looked as he marched across the food plot. At that point, he was about 80 yards away. I grabbed my grunt call and grunted once. The buck whipped his head around and saw my decoy. He immediately started toward it. As he got closer, I could see just how big he really was. Later I would find out that this deer weighed 215 pounds dressed out, without a hide, head, or feet. He had to weigh more than 300 pounds. The inside spread of his rack was more than 22 inches.

Imagine a deer of that caliber walking up on my ratty little one-horned decoy. Without a doubt, he must have believed the fight wouldn't last long. Once he reached 20 yards, I came to full draw. When I hit the trigger on my release, the spray of water looked like a heavy fog because of all the moisture soaked into my bowstring. The buck ran about 60 yards and stopped. I could tell I had hit him, and it wasn't long before he went down.

I stood in awe of what had just happened. After 12 hours in the most miserable conditions possible, I had done it. The Velcro buck was dead. He was so big, I had to go get my hunting buddies to help me drag him out. All they could say was, "Dude, you deserve this deer. We don't know of a single hunter who is hunting today, but you stuck it out."

This story is my best example of going the extra mile while hunting. I was cold, wet, tired, and mentally spent, but before the hunt even began, I had decided not to give up. I really believe this is one reason I have enjoyed so many successful hunts. I love playing the chess game. Of course, I don't always win, but when I do, it's worth every ounce of effort. So go to the next mountain. Stay in the stand a little longer. Practice a few more shots. It will be worth it.

Four days after the a debacle with the Velcro Buck, David got a rare second chance and took him from a different stand on the same farm.

DAVID'S LIFE TIP

The Extra Mile Is Never Crowded

Going the extra mile while hunting is one thing, but what about going the extra mile in life? When I was a fire department captain, I kept my crew at the training tower a little longer than most. I wanted to make sure my guys were as prepared as possible. Years later, I am still the guy who is always overpreparing for life. When I leave this earth, I want people to be able to say that I put my full effort into everything I did.

I think becoming a go-the-extra-mile person takes time, and you have to be willing to learn along the way. I recall trying to teach Warren the importance of giving life all you've got and not knowing whether he truly understood what I was trying to explain. The occasion was his first-ever elk hunt.

We hunted elk in an area in Montana that was at least six miles off the main road. The only way to reach it was on what I would describe as a bicycle path. The problem was, it was uphill the entire way in. When I was in the best shape of my life, I took just more than an hour to peddle my bike the six miles to my hidden hunting spot. It was a torturous journey. Coming out, however, was the fun part. With one peddle of my bike, I could fly down the hill in 20 minutes.

Warren was 13 at the time, and thanks to his grandparents (who went the extra mile spoiling our boys by feeding them Hershey bars after school every day), he wasn't in the best of shape. I was apprehensive about taking him that far off the main road, but he was adamant about going, and he assured me that he was prepared for the long ride in.

The day of Warren's introduction to elk hunting arrived. I had anticipated that we would need a little extra time, so we left two and a half hours early. We were in full hunting gear with our bows strapped to our backs, and high temperatures made the six-mile bike ride even more difficult. At the two-hour mark, we weren't quite halfway. I was now worried that we were about to make a huge mistake because the bicycle trail ended in the meadow we would be hunting. If we arrived at sunset, elk would most likely already be feeding in the meadow. If we spooked them, our chances of harvesting a bull would be greatly reduced over the next three days.

Warren's lack of physical training and his poor eating habits caught up with him. I tried explaining the importance of picking up our pace, but Warren wanted to stop peddling and walk our bikes the rest of the way in. I told him at this point we only had two choices: We could hurry and hunt, or we could turn around and go back.

Warren wasn't about to turn around. He hopped back on his bike and gave me the extra I had asked him for. Through tears, he pushed himself forward, and we made it to our hunting camp before the elk were in the meadow. One of my best memories is of Warren sitting next to our little tent with a proud smile on his face. He could have given up and turned around, but instead, he chose to push ahead.

The next few days weren't easy for him, and he was frustrated by the fact that it was much easier for me to navigate the difficult terrain. Warren got to experience firsthand the difference between someone who had been going the extra mile for years and someone who was going the extra mile for the first time.

Warren didn't kill a bull on that trip, but in my book, it was a success. He learned something more valuable on that mountainside than how to gut an elk. He learned how to give life all you've got. The entire ride home, all he could talk about was how he had made it in there and how he had almost killed a bull. This was one instance in which I was glad I had pushed him. I had to encourage him to fight hard for what he wanted by leaving nothing in the tank. Now, almost a decade later, that same hunting trip still lights a fire under him. He wants to go back and hunt that same spot. Only this time things will be very different as Warren is now in far better shape than I was the day of that hunt.

As much as I love the thought of Warren going back and killing a giant bull, I'm even more excited about watching him use what he learned while he was there to succeed in other areas of his life. Without any training, he recently built our new *Raised Outdoors* smartphone app. Seeing him struggle through the beginning of the process was a lot like watching him try to ride his bike up the mountain when he was 13 (without the tears). Warren doesn't know how to quit, and I like to think he learned that from Karin and me.

Going the extra mile in one area can teach you to go the extra mile in other areas as well. Like Warren, you can find yourself in the place you've only been dreaming about and be further down the road than you ever imagined. The extra mile is sometimes torturous. And in my opinion, that's why it's never crowded—but it will take you to the places most never see. You can be an extra-mile spouse, parent, friend, hunter, and lover of God. The choice is yours.

DAVID'S FAITH TIP

Be an "Extra-Mile" Follower of Christ

I used to think I wasn't qualified to teach anyone how to be an ultimate Christian hunter. But I've come to realize that in my relationship with God, I don't have to be perfect. He doesn't expect me to be flawless. He just wants me to do my best by striving to put Him first. I wish I could say I always do that. I don't, but I'm always trying.

As I reflect upon our *Raised Hunting* show, I can think of moments when I was giving God credit without even realizing it. God has been working through me in ways I haven't always paid attention to. God has been going the extra mile for me for years, even when I wasn't doing the same for Him. He has allowed me to go on spectacular hunting trips and to be a part of things that He would one day use for His glory. Karin and I have certainly lived our lives to the fullest, and God is using all our experiences in ways we never could have imagined.

In the early days, we weren't thinking about *Raised Hunting* or what it would be like to share our family with the world, but God was. You may not feel as if your life is very exciting, but you can be confident that God is going the extra mile for you and that He will fulfill His purpose in you. If God can spread His Word through me, even when I had no clue what He was doing, then He can do the same for you.

Our television show has opened doors for us that we never could have opened without God's help. Without a doubt, *Raised Hunting* paved the way for our hunting camps, Raised at Full Draw. We go the extra mile by unapologetically being who we are at camp. We include prayer, and we honor this great country that we live in by starting each day with the pledge of allegiance. We have church. We take the time to thank God for what He has done for us. We realize that the animals we get to hunt come from Him and that we should always be grateful.

If anything in this life deserves your best, God does. I see a lot of people giving everything they've got while hunting. I commend them for their effort, but I wonder how much time and energy they are giving God. Are they pursuing Him with the same intensity as they pursue animals?

Jesus can make a huge difference in your life. I know, because I'm the guy who's been on both sides of the fence when it comes to having a relationship with Him. If you haven't yet allowed God to have full control of your life, trust me, I can relate. But when I wasn't going the extra mile to find Him, He was going the extra mile to find me. And He is going the extra mile to find you. Just the fact that you are reading this book proves that Jesus loves you and knew that one day you would be flipping through these pages. Jesus went the extra mile for you by giving His life, and you can go the extra mile for Him by giving Him yours. Don't wait like I did. Pursue Him with your whole heart today.

Love the Lord your God with all your heart and with all your soul and with all your mind and with all your strength.

MARK 12:30

THERE'S NO CURE FOR BUCK FEVER
Control yourself, and you'll control the shot.

Nothing compares to the unbelievable surge of adrenaline you experience when a giant buck is approaching. All of us who love deer hunting get buck fever. Hands shaking, heart pounding, heavy breathing, and in severe cases, the lack of normal brain function…these are only a few of the symptoms a hunter can experience once the fever hits.

During my years of hunting, guiding, and filming, I've seen the most hardcore hunters lose their composure. Buck fever can lead to wounded or missed animals, confusion about how the missed shot occurred, and even tears. Personally, I've suffered from the extreme excitement that comes right before launching an arrow. Buck fever is real, and I don't want it ruining my next hunt—or yours.

It's tough for any hunter to perform accurately and efficiently when a big buck, bull elk, or gobbling turkey is within range. The last thing you want is for shaky nerves to blow your chances when the animal you've prepared for finally shows up. Several years ago, I began trying to figure out how to calm myself in that anxious moment right before the shot.

My solution came by surprise as a deer I had been praying for slowly approached my setup. The season had been particularly rough, without many opportunities, so I was already more anxious than usual. For whatever reason, when the big buck reached 60 yards from my location, I began telling myself he wasn't going to come close enough for a shot.

But he kept coming. He was walking straight toward me, and in just a few seconds, he was at 30 yards. But after all the previous failures, I wasn't ready to get my hopes up just yet. I began telling myself, *This buck is never going to turn broadside.*

Suddenly, he switched trails and was now broadside at 15 yards. Then I thought, *He's too close—I'll never get to full draw.* Before I knew it, I was at full draw and looking at the buck through my peep sight. At this point, autopilot kicked in, and I made a soft doe bleat. The buck stopped broadside at 12 yards. I settled my pin behind his shoulder and made the perfect shot. It only took a few seconds for the giant Montana whitetail to tip over.

After he was down, a huge surge of shaking and an uncontrollable feeling of appreciation came over me. My knees became weak as I tried to process what had just happened. Then I realized how calm I had been right up until the moment of the shot. I had managed to completely control myself. I was able to calmly reach full draw just by telling myself that it wasn't going to happen. This allowed me to settle my pin on the big deer and squeeze the trigger on my release without hesitation or mistake. I hadn't stopped the buck fever (nor would I want to), but I had simply held it off until after I had harvested the buck.

Buck fever is one of the many things that make deer hunting so exciting and addicting. However, learning to control when and how it shows up will increase your chances the next time that buck you've been dreaming of makes an appearance.

STEALTH CAM   11:11 AM 11/11/19   4 °F   ●   RAZED23 CAM

Bucks like this can cause permanent buck fever!

ENCOURAGEMENT FROM KARIN

Be the Hunter, Not the Hunted

> *Be alert and of sober mind. Your enemy the devil prowls around like a roaring lion looking for someone to devour.*
> **1 PETER 5:8**

Animals are fascinating. I never grow tired of watching them or discovering their own unique ways of defending themselves against predators. Skunks put off a terrible odor when threatened, while porcupines have quills that keep a predator from snatching them up. Whitetail deer have keen senses of smell and sight, and their response time is amazing. All three of those animals know exactly what to do if they want to avoid becoming a snack.

However, when a predator is really hungry and needing to fill its stomach, it will often sit back to watch and wait patiently—hoping to capture its prey in a moment of weakness or perhaps when it lets down its guard.

When we were living in Montana, a hungry mountain lion had crept to within a very short distance of our home to watch the deer grazing in our yard. A lion like this one is patient and full of stealth. It will often sit motionless for hours, waiting for the right moment to pounce on its prey. I remember the day that opportunity presented itself and the lion attacked, killing a deer and dragging it off into the nearby timber to feed. Having lived in mountain country, I knew the big cat would find a safe place to fill its belly and then bury the rest to eat later. Not wanting this dangerous predator anywhere near our home, I loaded my 12-gauge shotgun and went looking.

Warren and Easton were just boys at the time, and since David was out of town, I took them with me as I tracked the lion. With every step, we became more and more nervous, but we were determined to get the lion away from our home. I wanted to make sure the killer cat was gone and not coming back anytime soon. As we followed the enormous paw prints laced with deer hair, my heart was beating out of control. The hair on the back of my neck was standing up, and I was breathing hard. I prayed the entire time that the Lord would keep us safe.

God answered my prayer and kept His promise to watch over and protect us. We eventually found a half-eaten deer carcass buried in a fresh mound of dirt. I was certain the lion would return in a day or two to finish his meal. We destroyed his hiding spot in order to discourage his return. Thankfully, we never saw him again.

Satan is a lot like that mountain lion. He too is crafty. Satan studies our weaknesses and watches our every movement, waiting for a good opportunity to pounce just like the lion pounced on that deer. Satan is always looking for an access point into our lives. Once he finds an opening, he will begin to cloud our minds with lies or perhaps dig in his claws, stirring up old hurts from the past. And just like with the deer in our yard, he needs us to let down our guard so he can come charging in to devour. Lions often blend into their surroundings in order to make the kill, and Satan will do the same. He will sneak in, possibly in the form of someone or something you never saw coming. This is one of his best tricks, and it's designed to keep you from trusting in God's promises.

Everyone has moments when they feel weak and susceptible to the enemy's attack. That's why the apostle Peter told us to stay alert and sober. To be safe from the lion, you must first learn to recognize when the lion is watching you. Don't make the same mistake that deer in my backyard made. All the lion needed was for her to let down her guard for a few minutes.

Now would be a good time for you to evaluate your own life. Do you have cracks or doors that you have left open where the lion can creep in? Are you ready to close those openings in your life so that you don't end up as lion food?

REFLECTION

If you feel as if Satan is pursuing you, what will you do today to stop him?

The Lord is faithful, and he will strengthen you
and protect you from the evil one.
2 THESSALONIANS 3:3

9

EXPERIENCE IS THE BEST TEACHER

DAVID'S PRO TIP

Let Them Learn

I've always been the guy who jumps right in to get the ball rolling. Sitting back and watching while others are learning is unnatural for me. It wasn't until four or five years ago that I realized how my eagerness to assist was sometimes holding back the people closest to me. Here's an example.

I was surprised one day to hear Karin say, "If you don't stop doing stuff for me while we're hunting, I'm never going to learn."

That was a hard pill to swallow because I love Karin and I'm always happy to help her. But she was right. I was always stepping in at the last second when I saw something that I believed wasn't going to work in her favor. I never gave her the space she needed to figure out what to do when something wasn't going as planned. I was the one making that final call to the big gobbler coming over the ridge. I was the one stopping the deer in the perfect spot for a clean shot. I was doing all the things I should have trusted Karin to do. I was definitely overstepping, but at the time, I thought I was helping.

The day Karin pointed this out to me, we were hunting in a deer stand not far from our house. On this hunt, we were trying to kill a doe. I love doe hunting, and to me, killing a doe (or any animal for that matter) is just as exciting as killing a big buck. I can honestly tell you that I still get the shakes every time a hunting partner or I prepare to harvest any deer.

On this day, a doe appeared, and it looked as if Karin was going to get a shot. As soon as the deer crossed into an opening, I gave a quick "meh," and the doe stopped. I looked over at Karin who was now at full draw, but she was not shooting. I waited, but Karin never released the arrow. Finally, the doe began to stomp her feet and then left the area. After letting her bow down, Karin turned to me and said, "What in the world were you doing?"

"What do you mean?" I replied.

"Why did you stop the deer?" she asked.

Karin explained that even though I had a clear view of the deer, she did not. She went on to say that it was her responsibility to stop the deer, not mine. I had just taken an opportunity to harvest a deer away from my wife even though I was trying to help.

Many of us hunters do that more than we realize, especially with our wives and kids. Too often, we step in and never allow them to learn the skills necessary to be an ultimate hunter without our help. By doing everything for them, we are not teaching them. Karin would have learned more that day by stopping the doe on her own. But I never even gave her that opportunity.

Over the course of our next few hunts, I had to pay attention to what I was doing and to what I needed to stop doing. I backed off considerably, but I was still helping her with her game calls. I have more experience than Karin using calls, and I was trying to show her how to effectively use them without repeating my habit of stepping on her toes.

Once again, we were on a deer hunt, and this time our stands were strapped to the same tree. Just like before, Karin was the shooter and I was filming. Karin's stand was facing the field where we believed the deer would cross, and my stand was facing the woods. Every deer we had seen that day was crossing on my side of the tree before working a scrape. We had seen four or five bucks, but none of them were giving Karin an opportunity to even attempt a shot.

I looked to my left and saw a shooter buck. He was following the same path as the other bucks and was heading straight to the scrape. I told Karin to grab her rattling antlers because there was a big buck in the woods. Karin whispered back that she hadn't brought any rattling antlers with her. Trying not to spook the buck, I told her to use her grunt call, which she did. Karin grunted a couple of times, but the buck was about 60 yards away and walking through the leaves, so he never heard her.

I immediately told her she would have to snort wheeze because we needed something louder. What I didn't know was that she didn't have the kind of call that could produce a snort wheeze.

I was getting frustrated, and even though I had a snort wheeze call, I didn't use it because I wanted Karin to do this on her own. To my surprise, Karin decided to attempt a snort wheeze on her grunt call! Now, if you've ever tried that, you already know how funny that sounds. It sounded more like an angry bear with hiccups than a buck looking for a fight. I was startled and caught completely off guard.

I turned to Karin and said, "What in the world was that?" To my surprise, as she was explaining to me that she didn't have a snort wheeze call, I looked up and saw the buck coming straight toward us. I was in shock and wondered what in the world Karin had just said to him with that weird sequence of grunts. Upon closer inspection, I realized that this was not the same buck I had seen earlier. This guy was much bigger, and he was walking straight at us.

The buck got to within 17 yards, and I was telling myself not to stop him. I had to trust Karin to do it herself. With a "meh," Karin stopped the buck. But there was a problem. The buck was facing us, so she did not get a shot. To this day, Karin is not upset about not harvesting that buck because she learned a valuable lesson. Karin didn't fail—she just figured out what not to do when a big buck is walking straight toward you.

My point is, once your hunting partners have the fundamentals of hunting down, let them learn on their own. Let them nock their own arrow. Let them set up their own ground blind. Let them put on their release and safety harness. You can check to make sure they're safe, but you don't need to do it for them. At first, you may not come home with as many deer or turkeys, but you will come home with a more experienced and ready hunter. In my book, that's more important than filling a tag.

HUNT THE WEATHER

A break in the weather tips the scales in your favor.

The rain had not let up for more than 24 hours, and no matter how many times I checked the big green blob on the radar, it kept coming down. But a break was coming, and I was urging my family to have their hunting gear gathered and ready. I knew that once the front finally passed over, we would need to be in our tree stands as soon as possible.

As usual, my family told me to relax, reminding me that it was just noon and that the deer wouldn't be moving for another couple of hours.

I replied, "You guys don't understand. When the rain quits, it won't matter what time it is because the deer activity will be off the charts." I was frantic (even though the drive to our farm was less than 15 minutes). Eventually, they agreed to head out earlier than we had planned, and as we were driving, the clouds began to break up. I told Karin that once we arrived, we needed to hurry.

When we got there, the boys went to one stand and Karin and I headed to another. Before we could even get to the tree, we saw two bucks chasing a doe. Karin now understood my urgency and was in high gear, and in less than ten minutes, we were in our stand and ready to hunt.

As always, the plan was to begin the hunt with an opening interview for our show, but before we could get started, I spotted a big buck passing by at 75 yards. Karin quickly grabbed her rattling antlers and crashed them together. Before she had time to set them down, the cruising buck had closed the distance and was now standing below us at less than 10 yards. Karin killed her first nontypical Iowa buck that day, but more importantly, she saw firsthand how significant a passing weather front can be while hunting whitetails.

Many things affect whitetail deer movement, including cold weather, high pressure, moon phases, and even crops being harvested out of a feeding area. But nothing sparks deer movement more than a break in foul weather. In my experience, the longer the weather has held them in place and the faster the weather improves, the more the deer will move. If a weather front moves out of the area but is replaced by high winds, deer movement will be slow. But if the weather conditions go from bad to really good in a short time, watch out! The day Karin shot her deer is a perfect example. I've rarely seen such a dramatic change in the weather, and when it switched from rain to calm, the deer didn't care about the time or temperature. They had been hunkered down and were now ready to be out and about.

The boys also saw more than 20 deer from a stand that was deep in the timber. As we drove home, they asked me how I knew the deer were going to move like that.

"Redneck gut feeling, I guess."

Easton said, "If you ever get that feeling again, please tell me! That way I won't have to get up at 4:30 anymore. We can just wait until every deer in the country is moving and go hunt then!"

The next time you look at the weather and think it might not be worth going hunting due to rain or snow, think again. You can actually maximize your time if the weather breaks. An hour of hunting after a hard rain can be more productive than an entire day spent in one of your best locations.

DAVID'S LIFE TIP

Life Is a Lesson

Learning on your own is not the same as mimicking what someone else is telling you. I'm not saying you can't learn from instruction, but there are some things that require a more hands-on approach. In life as in hunting, you need more than a voice telling you what to do. You need to be willing to jump in and give it your best shot, even if you completely miss the target the first time.

Karin and I have raised two boys, and even though they are grown and out of the house, we still catch ourselves trying to figure out life for them. I don't ever want to stop being their dad, but I realize that I can no longer treat them the way I did when they were little. And that means that sometimes I have to let them struggle and learn on their own because if I continue to step in and do it for them, I will end up creating adults who don't know how to overcome life's obstacles.

As much as I love life, I can tell you that it is no cakewalk. Things will happen that you don't see coming, and how you handle those things will determine whether you move on fairly well or crash. I want Warren and Easton to know what to do when life takes what looks like a wrong turn.

If you think you can always cover all the bases for your kids, you're kidding yourself. You can't. There is no way to protect them from every potential obstacle. What you can do is teach them values, responsibility, good work ethics, the difference between right and wrong, and how to make beneficial choices. I know how hard it is to watch your kids struggle, especially when you believe you have a way to help them get out of that struggle. When tempted to rescue our boys, I have to remind myself that I am who I am today because of the things I was forced to figure out on my own. Like it or not, that's how life works.

After Warren graduated from high school, he went through a time of believing he knew more than Mom and Dad. I think that's pretty normal for most kids. He came up with the bright idea that he was going to move to Des Moines, Iowa. We live out in the country about

40 miles from there, but Warren wanted his own apartment. It was difficult for me not to tell him how crazy I thought his idea was. Having spent the previous 18 years with him, I knew how much he loved living in the country and how cramped he would feel in a tiny apartment. I understood what it was like living in a big city, but Warren had no clue. When he approached me with the idea, as much as I wanted to tell him not to do it, I told him to go for it if that was what he wanted.

So Warren moved to the city. On his very first night, he had to sleep on the porch of his apartment because the air conditioning wasn't cooling it down enough. To make matters worse, his apartment complex was right on the interstate, so the noise of the traffic was unbearable. Warren had gone from living in the tranquility of the country to living in the chaos of the big city. Instead of hearing turkeys gobbling, all he could hear was horns honking!

To be honest, I wanted to call him the next day and ask if he was ready to move back home, but I didn't. Instead, I decided to let my son learn this lesson on his own. Sure enough, in a short time, he called to see if I knew anything about getting out of a lease agreement for an apartment. Everything inside me wanted to help him get out of that lease, but I didn't.

That was four years ago, and even though Warren struggled for a while, I'm thankful that I allowed him to learn the hard way. He now lives about 20 miles from us and has no interest in big-city living. I truly believe Warren made a mistake moving to the city, but that mistake helped him appreciate the environment where we live (and where he grew up) more than he ever did. As I write this, Easton is going through some of the same things his brother did, and it's just as hard for me not to step in.

Keep in mind that whether you're hunting or raising kids, sometimes you just have to let people stumble. You made mistakes in your life too, and you turned out okay. As much as you love them, you have to give them a chance to figure it out on their own—just like you did.

The Holder family has learned that hard lessons can either bring us down or build us up. The choice is ours.

DAVID'S FAITH TIP

You Can't Do It for Them

My family didn't attend church regularly while I was growing up. My parents will tell you that when it came to going to church, our family could take it or leave it. We didn't avoid going, but we didn't practice going. As a result, I didn't have a solid platform for living out my faith. I'm not blaming my parents for my lack of understanding, because they were only doing what they felt was best for me at the time. As a young man, I always believed in God but was never interested in making Him a daily part of my life or seeking His direction. It wasn't until after I met Karin that I discovered that some people went to church all the time—people who included God in their regular, everyday lives.

In the beginning of our marriage, I tried to go to church with Karin, but to be honest, I didn't enjoy it. I won't go into the details, but the church she was attending at the time left me feeling beat up. I left there thinking I could never be good enough to go to heaven. We no longer attend that kind of church, and now I feel like I have a good handle on my relationship with God. I know that He loves me despite all the reasons I sometimes give Him not to. Jesus doesn't beat me up—He lifts me up.

Teaching someone to hunt while allowing them to learn it for themselves is a lot like helping someone grow as a Christian. You can't live out someone's faith for them, but you can coach them along the way. I wish I had met someone when I was younger who would have pointed me in a better direction and helped me build a solid relationship with God. Thankfully, I met Karin, and she filled that role.

In the early years of our marriage, Karin guided me in my relationship with God the way I guided her in hunting. At first, she wanted to do it for me, believing that if I went to the same church she did and followed her lead, I would be in the same spiritual place as she was. But we quickly found out that wasn't going to happen. She had to back off and allow me to learn on my own. Just as I had to let her make a few mistakes while hunting so that she could learn, she had to allow me to fail a few times so that I could learn.

Regardless of how good a hunter I might have been, Karin had to do more than just watch. And no matter how good a Christian she might have been, I had to do more than just watch. With hunting and with Jesus, you can't do it for them, but you can do it with them.

If anyone would come after me, let him deny himself and take up his cross and follow me. For whoever would save his life will lose it, but whoever loses his life for my sake will find it.
MATTHEW 16:24-25 ESV

ENCOURAGEMENT FROM KARIN

Lost

> *Without faith it is impossible to please God, because*
> *anyone who comes to him must believe that he exists*
> *and that he rewards those who earnestly seek him.*
> **HEBREWS 11:6**

I knew we had walked by the same tree at least twice before, but I just kept walking. Kristi (my best friend) was following behind me. She wasn't worried. And why would she be? After all, she trusted our guide to get us out of the Canadian bush. Kyle, my cameraman, was also with us. I could tell by the look on Kyle's face that he too was beginning to question whether we were going in the right direction. And to be honest, I was beginning to wonder if the bear hunt we had just been on was going to turn into us being hunted!

One of the hunters in our camp had taken a shot at a bear but was not confident that he had hit the animal well enough for a quick kill. As a result, we were part of a team of people out looking for his bear. With our guide leading us, we had all been walking in the same area for quite some time. I trusted his course, but it felt to me as if we were walking in circles. So I started to pray. *Okay, Lord, I think we're lost. Maybe You could help with some directions. Please...*

I didn't want to embarrass the guide, so I jokingly asked if we were turned around. "A little bit," he replied. Cell phone service is nonexistent in the area we were hunting, so the GPS on our phones wasn't working. And no one had a Garmin GPS, which connects to satellites. All we could do was look at the position of the sun in the sky to determine the direction we were headed.

Suddenly I remembered that two other hunters were also searching for the bear. They weren't with us, but maybe they were close. We began to holler for them, and sure enough, we got an answer. We continued to yell until we got close enough to walk out into the meadow where we had left our trucks a few hours earlier. We got back to our camp safe and sound and were lost for only a couple of hours. However, I will admit it was scary. I don't like being lost or the feeling of not knowing exactly where I am.

Just like on this bear hunt, it's easy to get lost in life. You can get turned around in a very short amount of time. Lost and confused, you walk in circles, wondering where in the world you're going. You ask yourself, *What is my purpose, and what am I supposed to be doing to accomplish that purpose?* It can even take you a while to realize that you are lost. Just as I had to pass by the same tree two or three times before it began to dawn on me that I was walking in circles, life has a way of spinning you around until you've lost all sense of direction.

Fortunately for us, we have a place to go with our chaos and confusion. We have Jesus, a solid rock to lean on when we need direction and understanding. I think we have to be careful during those times when we aren't quite sure where we're at, not to turn to artificial escape routes. The enemy also offers us a way out, but his path takes us deeper into the wilderness and never truly leads us out. And while those alternative routes might seem like better options at the time, they never take us anyplace worth going. Bad choices create pain and a ripple effect of destruction.

While hunting, I'm usually confident that with enough time, I can find my way. But in life, I've learned that without God's help, finding my way is impossible. Turning my worries over to Him and then listening to His directions is the only way I can succeed. Jesus isn't just a destination. He is the way…He is constant and never changing.

REFLECTION

In what areas are you trying to find your own way or blaze your own trail? How will you realign yourself with God's path?

10

LEARN FROM YOUR MISTAKES

Mistakes Make Us Better Hunters

A successful hunt doesn't always end with a skillet full of backstraps. Sometimes it's our failure to get it right that teaches us to become better hunters. This was the case with Warren and me on an elk hunt in the backcountry of Montana. He and I were hunting on public land that I knew very well. Having hunted there many times over the years, I was certain the elk would be plentiful, and I felt confident that Warren's chances of harvesting a bull were pretty high. I've already mentioned parts of this story in a previous chapter, but there were many lessons that Warren and I learned on this particular hunt, and I think it's important to give you a few more of the details.

Like I said, getting to where I knew the elk would be was no easy task. The terrain was rugged. Warren was 13 at the time, and this was his first elk hunt. He could have hunted elk when he was 12, but I wanted him to have more experience in the woods and be able to pull more poundage with his bow. It's important not to force an inexperienced hunter before they are ready.

Elk hunting is special to me, and I couldn't wait to share the experience with Warren. In my opinion, hunting elk has a profound effect on a human being. Maybe it's how big they are. Or perhaps it is how adrenaline begins flooding your body when you call to them and they answer. One thing is for sure: When an animal of that size closes the gap between you and what would be considered a safe distance, there's no other feeling like it. Getting an elk at less than 30 yards (because at the time, that was as far as I felt comfortable allowing Warren to shoot) would be no easy task. Even if everything went perfectly, there were still no guarantees.

My plan was to bike most of the six miles to our hunting grounds, set up our camp, and hike to where I had seen numerous elk earlier that same year. I allowed two extra hours for Warren to make his first-time trek into these mountains. It turned out to be a good decision, as he found it to be far more grueling than he expected. The ride in was all uphill, and at one point, Warren was ready to quit.

We were way behind schedule and on the verge of spooking the elk we had come there to hunt. I explained to Warren that we could either hurry and get there or turn around and go back. I emphasized how it was close to dark and how the herd would soon be in the area. If we spooked them, they would be gone, and our hunt would be over before it even started. Warren understood the seriousness of the situation and dug deep. We made it in without spooking the elk.

Now we were in the right place, but for whatever reason, it was the wrong time. The elk I had previously seen in this area were nowhere to be found. Spending three days looking for an elk was not what I had planned on, but it was what was happening on this hunt. We had only a few random encounters with the elk we were hunting, and it began to take its toll on us both. Finally, on the last day, I looked down into a meadow and saw three small bulls feeding on the lush grass. I told Warren our chances were good and that it was time to finally get him in position to take one of those bulls. All we had to do was walk half a mile and ensure the wind would not blow our scent out into the meadow and alert the bulls to our presence. We went for it.

We came down the mountain to where the bulls should have been, but we could no longer see exactly where they were. The meadow was mostly open, so our only hope of getting one of those elk close enough to shoot was to position Warren at the edge of the meadow behind a tree. I would lie flat on my gut well behind him to call. If everything came together the way we had planned, it would work. Now all we had to do was pick the tree and get set up.

At that point, I decided to do something that still haunts me to this day. I thought our best bet was to sneak to the top of the little rise in front of us, spot the elk, back up, and then call. That was our plan. As we crept forward, we didn't make it more than 40 yards before I saw antlers coming over the hill. The only thing we could do was quickly jump up and run back to our tree, so that's what we did. Warren was beaming with excitement, as he could now see the elk. For the first time on this hunt, things were looking up. All I had to do was make the first cow call, and they would start coming his way.

With the first call, I got the attention of a young bull. He squealed out his best bugle and began walking toward us. I could barely take my eyes off Warren's face. My heart practically swelled outside of my body at the excitement in his eyes. I could see the steam of his breath as the bull came closer—and closer still. Now the elk had closed the distance to about 40 yards, and I saw that he was going to come to the right side of the tree. I motioned to Warren what was about to happen, and he moved his bow perfectly to the other side of the tree without being spotted by the bull. Everything was working perfectly—or so we thought. Suddenly, the elk stopped and, for no apparent reason, started running in the other direction. There was no way the elk could have seen Warren because of the size of the tree he was hiding behind, and the wind couldn't have busted us because it was blowing in our faces. So what had happened?

Then it hit me. The elk hadn't seen anything. He had smelled where Warren and I had been standing just a few minutes earlier. We had just made one of the biggest mistakes a hunter can make when stalking an animal that can smell you: walking up somewhere and then coming back to set up. Our scent was still very strong, and just like a dog tracking a person, the elk knew how recently we had been there. By stepping into the same spot where we had just stood ten minutes earlier, the elk received all the information he needed to get out of there in a hurry. So instead of watching my son take his first elk, I watched that elk run off over the hill. I can't express how sick I was about that and how horrible I felt for Warren. I explained to him the mistake we had made. It wasn't easy, but to this day, I will never forget the lesson I learned on that hunt. Warren has gone on to kill much larger elk than the one we messed up on, and if you asked him, he would tell you that part of the reason is because of what he learned from the mistake his dad made.

Making mistakes can make you a more successful hunter when you're careful not to repeat them. Just ask Warren.

Warren's 2014 bull reminds us that hard work and stick-to-itiveness will lead us to victories in life and on the mountain.

DAVID'S LIFE TIP

Mistakes Are Opportunities to Be More Successful

I wish I could tell you to go to the library and check out a certain book that contained all the information to solve your problems and eliminate all your mistakes—but it's not that simple. Life has a way of teaching you what you need to learn.

I haven't always been a TV producer or had one of the top-rated hunting shows. My life before all that was very different. During my 17 years as a firefighter/EMT, I learned the value of organization, attention to detail, commitment, loyalty, and trust—all things that I believe have contributed to the success of *Raised Hunting*. In my opinion, those who choose to fight for their country in the armed forces and those who protect others as civil servants often sacrifice the most. The hours are long, and the appreciation is short. These brave men and women are proud of what they do, and no matter how hard it is, they tirelessly absorb the pain around them so that others don't have to experience it. In those years, I saw and heard things that most people would try to block out, not to purposefully recall and write down in a book for the world to read.

Some would say that no matter how much you prepare for life, you will never fully be ready—but I'm not telling you that. I believe that God will put you in difficult places to prepare you for the life He has planned for you. That has always been the story of David Holder. Allow me to explain.

As a firefighter, I became proficient in auto extrication (cutting up cars and removing victims from the vehicle). In fact, the state of Montana hired me to teach that skill to others. Ironically, the reason I was so good is that when I first started, I was so bad!

Montana required all full-time and volunteer firefighters to become certified in auto extrication. A portion of that training meant that each firefighter had to go through a strict regimen of time drills to test proficiency at removing a patient from a vehicle. This included an exercise in which a three-man crew had a certain amount of time to remove all of a vehicle's doors, the windows, and the roof and then push the dashboard away from an assumed patient in the driver's seat. Most of the members of our department passed this test with a few tries, but the crew I was on was struggling. No matter what we did, we just could not get it right. We tried different techniques and different approaches, but each time, the result was the same—complete failure.

Then one of the instructors suggested that we work more as a team and less as individuals. He was right. Week after week and car after car, instead of working together, we had been working against one another. The answer was right in front of us the entire time, but we were too busy trying to accomplish our goal to see it.

On the next car we approached, we carefully planned our assignments. We decided who was going to go where, how they would get there, and what tools they would use. We planned not only for what should go right but also for what might go wrong. We had done it wrong so many times, creating a list of possible obstacles was easy.

We were finally ready. And when the instructor gave us the nod to begin, we looked like three grown men auditioning for *America's Got Talent*. Every move was orchestrated as if an actual patient were in the car. We knew our job was to save their life, which is exactly what we should have been doing in the first place. It was a thing of beauty— every cut and every tear was in the right place at the right time. Before we knew it, we had flawlessly removed the patient from the car in record time.

Even though we had not cooperated effectively in all the failed attempts, we had become extremely proficient with our tools. We had cut up more cars than anyone cared to admit, so we knew what to expect from the various car manufacturers. Regardless of the metal or plastic alloys we were facing, nothing could stop us. What happened in the days following our accomplishment was not expected and has stuck with me to this day.

I'm not sure whether the state felt sorry for me or if they truly believed I had turned a corner. Either way, they didn't just offer me a passing grade—they offered me a job. The same state that had watched my team struggle was now giving me the opportunity to teach what we had learned to other departments across the entire state of Montana!

I was asked to teach not only how to approach an auto extrication but how *not* to approach the extrication of a person from inside a vehicle. In their minds, I had more training than most at both.

It wasn't until I was standing in front of my first crew of students that I truly recognized what I had learned. I explained to them that I wasn't there to teach them how great I was at cutting up cars. Rather, I would teach them how bad I once was and how my crew overcame our mistakes by learning along the way.

The mistakes of your past don't have to be indicators of the future. If you learn from them, like me, you can regroup and become more, not less.

TAKE A KID HUNTING

It's never too early to get them started.

Karin, Warren, and I were creeping down a hill and doing our best not to make the slightest sound. A few minutes earlier, we had spotted a bull elk from across the ridge, and we hoped to get close enough for a better look. Like magic, the elk appeared and was standing less than 60 yards away. I asked Warren if he could see the bull. He didn't answer.

I should probably mention that Warren was only six months old at the time, and he was snuggled in the pack on my chest. But by the way Warren was staring, Karin and I were convinced that even at six months old, he could see the giant bull that was feeding in and out of the sunshine along the edge of the timber.

When people ask me how soon they should start taking their kids hunting, my answer has always been that it's never too early to get them started. However, I also believe that how you introduce them to hunting can influence their decision of whether to stick with it. I feel truly blessed because both Warren and Easton still hunt right alongside me. When you add Karin to the mix…that's something really special. I can't explain how much it means to me that my family is as passionate about the outdoors as I am.

By the time our boys were two years old, they were already shooting bows. However, they were not name-brand bows costing hundreds of dollars. I went to Walmart and bought them the best kids' bows with suction-cup arrows I could find. Once I noticed they were getting bored with the suction cups, I made some modifications. Taking a string from one of my bows, I cut it to fit the toy bows. Next, I took some of my old arrows and cut them down as well. Then I gave them one of my old targets. Now they were able to shoot with Mom and Dad, and to top it off, their arrows actually stuck in the target. I can still remember the smiles on their faces as they walked the three yards to the target to pull out the arrows. One arrow after another flew from their tiny little fingers, and with each arrow they launched, the cheering got louder and louder. To me, it felt like game seven of the World Series!

After a few years of toy bows, we bought them bows that they could not only shoot but also grow into. By the time they were ten years old, they could pull enough poundage to ethically dispatch a big-game animal, but it all started with those toy bows in the backyard.

Before we took them hunting with us, we went hiking so they could use their binoculars to look for animals. We also had them climb up into tree stands and sit in ground blinds before they were old enough to hunt. I prioritized bringing them with me whenever I could.

I still planned hunts without them, especially when it was going to be a long day. One of the biggest mistakes I see parents make when introducing their kids to hunting is "too much too fast." You don't want your kids to burn out or dread spending an entire day in the woods. So start slow and work your way up to those longer hunts.

You can also make it fun for them by bringing snacks and

warm clothes. Even if you're not seeing anything, point out everything, such as a colorful leaf or a cool cloud formation. Be willing to shoot even the smallest of animals when your kids are with you. They don't care how big the antlers are. On some of our most fun bowhunting adventures, we never saw the quarry we were after, but Warren and Easton were hooked anyway. From moose-poop fights, to dangling from a tree stand (with safety harnesses on), to driving down a dirt road with a pop in one hand and a cookie in the other, they had fun even if we didn't see an animal. If you love the outdoors as much as I do, share it with your kids. When I'm with Warren and Easton, it's perfectly okay with me if the only thing we're killing is time.

DAVID'S FAITH TIP

God Won't Hold Your Mistakes Against You

The biggest mistake of my life has nothing to do with my old job at the fire department or even with the failed attempt of our first hunting show, *Above the Rest*. My biggest mistake is that I spent years not allowing God into my life. I was really good at picking and choosing when I needed God and when I didn't. In crisis, I would pull Him close, but in comfort, I would push Him away. That was the old David.

Although I'm not exactly where I want to be in my relationship with God, I'm not where I used to be either. I'm paying attention to God's voice, and my belief system is much stronger these days. When I wasn't including God in my life every day, something was always missing. And no matter what I did or how much I accomplished in those days, there was still very much a space in my life that I could not fill up by my own effort. Now I know that the hole in my heart was cross-shaped and something that only Jesus could fill.

So here is my faith tip: Don't make the same mistake I did and wait until you have a need that is bigger than you before you reach out to God. I'm okay with saying that because my mistake has taught me that life doesn't work without God's help. I hope that, like me, you will do your very best to build a relationship with God that is based not on what you need Him to do, but on what He needs you to do. You can take your mistakes to God, and He will take you just like you are, mistakes and all.

The godly may trip seven times,
but they will get up again.
PROVERBS 24:16 NLT

ENCOURAGEMENT FROM KARIN

Where God Guides, He Provides

She gets up while it is still night; she provides food for
her family and portions for her female servants.
PROVERBS 31:15

For me, hunting is much more than just a hobby or activity that I enjoy. It's a way for me to contribute to my family by providing food for them. David and I count on the harvest of wild game every year to fill our freezer. And even though I could easily go to the grocery store to buy our meat, that wouldn't be nearly as fun as hunting whitetail deer or chasing an elk through the mountains.

I spend a lot of time in the woods hunting. It's not always easy or convenient, but I wouldn't have it any other way. This requires long hours before dawn and after dusk in a tree stand or navigating thick timber in pursuit of a potential meal. It takes an extreme amount of effort to provide food for my family in this nontraditional way. In my opinion, there's nothing better than sitting down to a meal that I was directly involved in providing. It makes me smile to see David and our boys enjoying what I worked so hard to bring to the table.

If you think about it, God does the same for us. He is working behind the scenes in the still of night or in the bright of day to provide and to deliver on His promises.

When David and I decided to move from the beautiful, untamed northwest of Montana to Winterset, Iowa, there were many things that needed to line up perfectly for everything to work out. Moving across town is one thing, but moving 1,500 miles away brings an entirely new set of problems. At the time, Easton was playing on a baseball team that was winning every game and had a chance to take the state title. So for him, moving was a big deal. And Warren was really into football. We would need to find the right school with a good football program so that Warren could continue to excel. Adding to the pressure, David had gone to a hunting lodge for eight weeks. Bottom line—we needed a miracle. We needed God to hear us and show us His path for our family.

I prayed and asked God to perfectly coordinate our steps. We had certain criteria that had to be met before we could take a chance on such a drastic move. That's when God stepped in. He began opening doors and checking all our boxes. At Winterset, we were able to buy a house with 50 acres in prime whitetail deer country, so we hunt on our own property. God also provided the calm that I needed in order to uproot our family. We also needed our house in Montana to sell, and once again, God provided a buyer. From my job at Edward Jones Financial to the people we met in Iowa, everything lined up perfectly with what I had prayed.

I couldn't help but wonder why God was being so generous to us and answering all our prayers so seamlessly. Now I realize it was because we trusted Him to provide the answers we needed instead of trying to force our own way. We believed that He would deliver, and He did! He removed all the barriers and helped speed up the process. That didn't mean there weren't obstacles to overcome or days of frustration due to the big change in our lifestyles. God, however, helped with that as well.

God provided for our family, and God can provide for your family as well. He's the God who keeps His promises!

REFLECTION

Are you struggling to trust God's plan for the future? How will you transfer the load onto Jesus's shoulders?

Come to me, all you who are weary
and burdened, and I will give you rest.

MATTHEW 11:28

11

MANAGE YOUR EXPECTATIONS

Pursue Excellence, Not Perfection

Having spent the past four decades living the outdoor lifestyle, I can tell you that certain aspects of what we do have gotten easier over the years. At this point in my life, I have a pretty good handle on the basics. I no longer struggle with shooting my bow, hanging a deer stand, or planting a food plot. If you've been hunting for any length of time, I'm sure you can relate. Your mistakes in the woods will be fewer as you become a more experienced hunter.

An ultimate hunter not only hunts well, but perhaps more importantly, they know how to treat someone they are hunting with who makes a mistake. Maybe the hunting partner hit the wrong call, can't find a tree stand, or goes down the wrong trail. How you handle their inability says a lot about the kind of hunter you really are. In my case, I'm usually hunting with my family, so the stakes are even higher. How I treat them affects not only our hunts but also our everyday relationships.

When something has gone wrong on a hunt, I have sometimes responded in a way that I later regretted. I've been the guy who has said,

"What in the world were you thinking?," "We don't hunt this way," and "This is not safe." My intentions may have been good, but I have treated some of the people closest to me as if they couldn't do anything right. My hope is that as you read this chapter, you will learn from my mistakes and not go down that same path.

As you already know, my family and I take our television show very seriously. From the very beginning, we decided our show would include more than just the killing of animals. Our goal has always been to tell stories about hunting and the outdoor lifestyle. For the Holders, a successful hunt isn't about the kill. It's about everything that leads us to that moment. As much as we believe in this approach to outdoor television, it does occasionally put us in a difficult spot with our sponsors because they are relying on us for results. Also, to be respected in the outdoor industry, you have to be able to hunt efficiently.

Obviously, we try not to make mistakes. I will admit that I'm not always the easiest person to deal with when it comes to how we approach the filming of a hunt. I'm the guy who is constantly checking on everyone I'm hunting with to make sure they have everything we need. Adding television cameras to the mix makes things even more complicated. My motto is "If you didn't film it, then it never happened." I'm always pointing out how important it is to create the right conditions to give ourselves the best opportunity to film a high-quality television program. As much as I hate to admit it, I sometimes forget that there have been times when I was the one who didn't do a very good job preparing for a hunt. This is the story of how being underprepared can lead to thoughts of divorce.

A few years ago, on November 7, Karin and I climbed into a tree stand. The weather had been brutally cold, and to make the conditions even more uncomfortable, I had been giving Karin grief over everything from rattling the wrong way to not bringing all her hunting gear to the tree stand. On this morning, the weather was better, and the hunting conditions were finally right. I had been watching this particular area, and I knew we were in the right place for Karin to kill a good buck.

It wasn't long before the deer began to show up. We could see several does and a small buck walking along the edge of the food plot. The sun was coming up, and the temperature was just cold enough for us to see the breath of the deer passing by. As the cameraman that morning, I was excited about getting some great footage. Sure enough, about 20 minutes later, I saw a really good buck.

At first, he was tucked behind a small cedar bush, but I could still see his every breath. All I could think about at the time was how great this camera footage was going to be. Before long, he walked right below our stand. Through the camera lens, I could see the sun glistening off his antlers. The scene was absolutely perfect. Karin stopped the buck before releasing her arrow. I heard it hit the deer but couldn't tell whether her shot placement was good. I swung the camera around to record the big grin on Karin's face. She was convinced the shot was perfect.

Suddenly I saw four letters on the display of my camera that no one ever wants to see, especially after their wife has just whacked a great whitetail—STBY, which means standby. I had never hit the record button. Karin had just killed the biggest deer of her hunting career, and the guy who was always barking orders at others had just forgotten to hit record. I immediately felt sick, remembering all the times I have told others how crucial it was that we don't make mistakes like this. I had no excuse. I knew how important it was to see the "record" light on the top of the display. I was so engrossed in watching the deer and counting Karin's chickens before they hatched, I didn't double-check the screen display.

When it comes to filming a hunt, there is no second take. So even though I wanted to celebrate with Karin, I had to tell her what I had done. We had zero footage of the buck she had just killed. Everything I had been preaching to her about hunting, she had just flawlessly done. The only person who had failed was me.

In that moment, I realized that we will continue to make big mistakes we hadn't planned on. The biggest takeaway for me on this hunt was this: When someone around me makes a mistake, I don't need to badger them or point it out. Because like me on that hunt, they will already feel bad enough. Hopefully, they will own their mistake and make the proper adjustments so it doesn't happen again. I was already beating myself up, and it wouldn't have helped the matter if someone pointed out my failure. That day changed me. Remembering my own faults has helped me to stop being so critical of others.

November 7 will go down in history for me as the day I didn't hit record. You undoubtedly look back on a day like that as well. I hope you will remember that the next time your wife forgets to pack enough lunch or one of your kids misses a turkey at ten yards!

On November 7, 2018, Karin did her job and made a perfect shot, but David will always remember it as the day he didn't hit "record."

DAVID'S LIFE TIP

Chase to Understand, Not to Win

I used to think I could do whatever I wanted. When I was in my twenties, I thought life was just about having fun and enjoying myself. I mistakenly believed that I had total control over everything I did and that I didn't really need to concern myself with consequences. I wish I could go back and tell my younger self a thing or two about how life really works.

I'm not proud of this, but there was a time in my life when everything was about alcohol. Now I realize how naive and selfish I was. I wasted ten years of my life being hungover, inconsiderate, and a real jerk. My behavior was rooted in selfishness and an unwillingness to see what I was actually doing to myself and, later, to my wife. I truly believed that the problems I encountered weren't my fault. If I was having difficulty, it was obviously someone else's fault. I was blind to my own failures.

When Karin and I moved from Virginia to Arkansas, we decided it was time for us to get married. I knew Karin was the one I wanted to spend my life with, so marrying her was easy. What wasn't so easy was *how* we would get married, because our families didn't get along at the time. Believe it or not, about four days after our move, we went couch shopping in Searcy, Arkansas, and ended up at the justice of the peace. I thought that while we were there, we should just go ahead and get married. Karin agreed. We couldn't wait to tell my parents, who were in town from Virginia helping us move.

That night, we met them and my uncle for dinner. I will never forget what happened next. After Karin and I showed off our wedding rings and announced that we were Mr. and Mrs. David Holder, my mom got up and walked out. I couldn't understand why she was so upset—I knew how much she loved Karin. To make a long story short, what my mom really wanted was to be a part of our wedding, and she felt cheated out of that chance. At the time, I couldn't understand why she felt that way, and unfortunately, my mom and I didn't even speak to one another for a couple of years.

I look back now and realize that even though Karin and I thought we were doing the right thing for everyone, we had made a huge mistake. We had failed my mom by not even inviting her to participate in our little ceremony. After all, she was right there, and we didn't even think to tell her that she was welcome to witness our marriage.

My point is this: You won't always do everything right while hunting, and you also won't always get it right in life either. I think the biggest mistake I made that day wasn't my decision to not invite my mom. Rather, it was not realizing how much she was hurt by being left out. I honestly didn't think about how hurt she would be, but based on her reaction, I should have figured it out right away. I was thinking that if she didn't support what we had just done, then too bad. I hadn't even stopped to consider why she felt that way. All I wanted to look at was my side of the story, and I never gave a second thought to her point of view.

I'm not sure when I finally turned the corner, but the day came when I realized why my mom was so upset. I'm sure it was about the time Warren and Easton came along. I know how upset I would be if either of them did that to Karin and me.

We're all going to do things we never intended. Things like forgetting to hit record while filming your wife taking her best buck or damaging your relationship with your mom by not inviting her to your wedding. But don't be the person who makes the mistake even bigger by not owning your contribution. Be the person who is quick to apologize and move on.

Obviously, Karin didn't divorce me for not getting that buck on camera. In fact, she hardly ever brings it up…unless she is hinting about that Jamaican vacation she's always wanted.

THE WALK-BY TECHNIQUE

If a gobbler won't come, make him think you're leaving.

I had thrown every call in the book at a big tom turkey that seemed to be glued to the hillside about 200 yards away. For more than an hour, I had tried everything from soft seductive purrs to cutting so sharp it could sever a finger. Even though he was gobbling back nearly every time I sent a call his way, he wasn't coming any closer. I was getting frustrated, and since it was near the end of the season, I told my cameraman it was time to try something different.

My plan was to try the walk-by technique—creeping past the gobbling tom, calling as you go, making him believe you're going to walk right by without stopping. When using this trick, rather than walking toward the bird, flank him from the side. If you can stay out of his line of sight as you move past, he just might come to investigate your sudden departure.

On this hunt, I stopped about every 20 yards to give the smart old tom another yelp or two, and every time, he gobbled back. It wasn't until my cameraman and I had made it about 100 yards up the fence line that I noticed the gobbler had changed locations. His gobbling was much closer. That's when I noticed the strutting tom about 80 yards ahead of us. We stood motionless until the bird strutted behind a few pieces of brush. Then we quickly sat down against the fence. I gave one or two soft yelps, and the big bird was on his way. The tom was convinced that he had to cut the hen off before losing her forever.

That turkey was good eating, and his 11-inch beard and spurs are in my collection. I believe that had we not made the move to walk by him, he would still be strutting his stuff somewhere today. That small addition of realism grabbed his attention. I sounded like a lovesick hen that was tired of waiting and beginning to lose interest.

I will add a word of caution: When trying this tactic, make sure you're in a safe area where no other hunter will mistake you for a real turkey. Also, keep in mind that you may get busted by a gobbler's keen eyesight. However, when nothing else works, this little trick can be the icebreaker you were looking for. When your calls aren't enough and your location isn't working, try the walk-by technique and see if you can unglue that stuck-in-the-mud tom.

DAVID'S FAITH TIP

Chase Jesus

If you're like me, you're doing the best you can to live a life that makes God happy—and I'm not talking about following a bunch of rules. As I've already explained, I tried going to a church where the only thing that seemed to matter was how well I complied with a list of demands. I'm human, and that means I'm going to mess up. I'm far from perfect, and that is why I need Jesus. His love for me isn't based on my performance or how many commandments I keep. Jesus loves me simply because He created me and I'm His child.

It's easy to beat yourself up for past failures. Of course, some stuff doesn't really matter, like trying to use a grunt call to create a snort wheeze or forgetting to hit record on the video camera. But other things are more important. You regret your actions and wish you could go back and undo them because of the hurt you caused to yourself and others. Let me remind you that God knew you would make those kinds of mistakes, and that's why He sent Jesus. My point is— it's okay. And you're okay. You don't have to be perfect for God to perfectly love you.

Don't get me wrong; I think you should do your best, but you're going to mess up from time to time. If you hold yourself to an impossible standard, there's a good chance you won't enjoy anything, including hunting. Beating yourself up over how you've behaved in the past is the best way to sabotage the future.

This book has been about becoming the ultimate hunter, but I think becoming the ultimate Christian is an even better goal. You do that by asking Jesus to forgive all your past failures and then forgiving yourself. When I think back to the day I didn't get Karin's deer on film, it still frustrates me, but it doesn't frustrate Karin, because she has forgiven me. Your relationship with God works the same way. What you're still reliving, He has already forgotten. And if He is no longer holding it against you, then you can stop holding it against yourself.

I really believe that if you learned a hard lesson from a time when you failed God, then it wasn't a complete waste. Just as you have to learn the hard way while hunting, you will sometimes have to learn the hard way in life. But those are lessons you will never forget.

When Warren and Easton were growing up, I didn't write them off when they fell down or got something wrong. Instead, I helped them up, dusted them off, made sure they knew what to do next time, and sent them on their way. God does the same thing for me, and He will do it for you too.

Jesus didn't give His life for perfect people. He gave His life for guys like me who have never been perfect. Because of Jesus, I have a place to take my failure, and you can take your failure to Him as well. If you've never invited Jesus into your heart by asking Him to forgive your sins, I would be glad to help you do that. I would never tell you what to believe—only that you can believe. If you're ready to believe, pray this prayer.

> Dear Jesus, I know that I have sinned. I need You to forgive me of those sins. I believe that You are the Son of God and that You gave Your life for me on the cross. Help me to forget about the mistakes of my past by focusing on the future that You have for me. From this day forward, I am Your child, and I am forgiven. Amen.

If we confess our sins, he is faithful and just and will forgive us our sins and purify us from all unrighteousness.

1 JOHN 1:9

ENCOURAGEMENT FROM KARIN

No Compromise

> Jesus was led by the Spirit into the wilderness to
> be tempted by the devil. After fasting forty days
> and forty nights, he was hungry. The tempter came
> to him and said, "If you are the Son of God, tell
> these stones to become bread." Jesus answered, "It
> is written: Man shall not live on bread alone, but on
> every word that comes from the mouth of God."
>
> **MATTHEW 4:1-4**

While shooting my bow, I often like to change things up. I do this by shooting from various distances and places. When I'm practicing, you'll likely find me up in a tree stand or tucked away in a ground blind. I'll do just about anything to improve my skills so that when the moment of truth comes with an animal, I'm prepared to make the best shot.

Here's an example. This morning, I was shooting my bow at 60 yards. For me, that is a long distance and not a shot I would take while hunting. So why would I practice at such a long range? David has taught me to practice shots that are longer or harder than what I would normally shoot while hunting. Then, when the time comes, the shorter-range shots will be much easier. I've also learned that even though I can hit a static target at 60 yards, I might not make a good shot at a living, moving animal at the same distance.

Several years ago, David and I were hunting elk in Montana. As we reached the top of a ridge, David stopped to call. He immediately got an answer. In a flash, we saw a good bull running in our direction. We quietly got in position. Anticipating that the elk would show up right in our laps, we readied ourselves for a quick and clean kill.

As we waited, I took out my range finder to determine the distance between where we were sitting and several nearby landmarks. I often do this to effectively judge how far I can accurately shoot an animal. That day, I picked out a cedar tree at about 40 yards. I had already made up my mind that I wasn't comfortable taking a longer shot. This bull needed to come at least that close before I would release an arrow.

The bull, which we named Crown Royal due to the configuration of his rack, passed by at 43 yards—three yards farther than my effective range. Now I had a decision to make. Should I raise the pin on my sight a tiny bit and let the arrow fly, or should I stick to my effective range of no more than 40 yards and let him pass? In my mind, the chances were pretty high that I could safely harvest this bull. However, to do that, I would have to compromise the standard I had set for myself. When I'm hunting, I'm often thinking about protecting God's creatures from a dumb move on my part. On that day, I was definitely weighing my options.

I chose not to shoot. I allowed the biggest bull of my career to walk in and then out of my life because of three measly yards. What I remember most is how the sunbeams were glaring off his rack as he wheeled around and ran over the hill. Immediately, I began to question myself. Had I done the right thing? Some would say I was crazy for not releasing an arrow that day, but I continue to believe I made the right choice. I avoided the temptation to shoot past my comfort zone…even if it was only three yards.

While fasting for 40 days in the wilderness, Jesus was also tempted. It's hard for me to imagine how hungry He must have been. His lack of food would have led to garbled thinking and physical weakness. Not to mention the fact that His mind was no doubt screaming at Him for nourishment and questioning why He wasn't eating. I think most of us would have grabbed the first thing we could have gotten our hands on and eaten. After all, when you're starving, it's easy to forget the reason you're fasting in the first place.

Obviously, my elk hunt and Jesus's confrontation with Satan are two completely different things. But I'm glad that like Jesus, I didn't break the promise I had made to myself. My flesh wanted to shoot that day, but I didn't.

It would have been easy for Jesus to falter and play into the hands of Satan. After all, we all need food. Because Jesus stood up to temptation, so can you.

REFLECTION

What is Satan offering you? Like Jesus, how will you say, "Not today, Satan!"

12

YOUR BUCKET LIST

Write It Down (in Pencil)

It's been said that as soon as you're born, you begin the process of dying. That's a grim description of the future if you ask me, and it's certainly not the Holders' approach to life. What if instead of being born to die, you were born to live? Karin and I believe in living to the fullest. We've always taught our boys not to sit back and settle for what life throws at them but to stand tall by going after their wildest dreams. We also believe that God created us to enjoy our time wherever we are—indoors or in the woods.

It's usually near the end of your life when you start thinking about the list of things you would have liked to do. I know that was the case with my dad. We get so busy trying to make a living that we forget about the important stuff we've never done but want to do before it's too late. I'm guessing that like most hunters, you have a bucket list of animals you've only dreamed of hunting.

One day, Karin, Warren, Easton, and I were sitting in the basement of our home, cleaning a few guns and talking about this very thing. Karin had been after me for some time to put together a hunting bucket list of my own. I assured her that I had no list because I was already living my dream by hunting with my family. Karin wasn't buying it, and neither were the boys. Warren thought a Yukon moose would top my list. Easton was convinced that filming me on a brown bear hunt would make the cut. They were both right, and they could have added a caribou and a Boone and Crockett whitetail.

I finally admitted that I did have a list but hadn't taken the time to write it. I promised Karin that I would because she wasn't taking no for an answer. She was worried that one day I would wake up not having done half the things I said I would. One of the many things I love about Karin is that her bucket list includes making sure I get to live out some of the things on mine. As I would soon find out, she was right. It was time to start filling up my bucket.

I've never considered myself a trophy hunter. I live by the rule that if it gets me excited, it gets an arrow. I will admit that I do dream of big deer just like everyone else. I think that's part of hunting. Now that I'd reached the age where I had fewer hunting days in front of me than I had behind me, it was time to take Karin's advice. If I wanted to kill a Boone and Crockett whitetail, I needed to go where this type of deer lived. Karin was convinced that the place to start filling my bucket was Kansas. I agreed.

I booked the hunt, but at the time, I had no way of knowing what the weather conditions would be like when I arrived. The forecast had been calling for a little bit of everything: tornados, hail, wind, and eventually snow. To me, it doesn't matter whether you travel from Iowa to Kansas or Toledo to Texas. It doesn't matter where you go or what you're hunting. It doesn't even matter what the weather is like. If you're living life and having fun, you've already won.

I couldn't have asked for better hosts than the boys at Prairie Storm. I was with a new outfitter in a new state, which means new friends, new ground, and several new viewpoints of God's handiwork. All I needed now was a new deer.

November weather in Kansas is unpredictable, and on this hunt, we had a flood. I needed the rain to stop, but it didn't look very promising. I learned a lesson that day. In life and in hunting, we envision the future and what we think it will be like, yet somehow we never envision the truth. I had seen myself sitting in a tree stand, but instead, I was walking the floors of a hunting cabin. I was ready to check a Boone and Crockett buck off my list, but at first, the rain wasn't ready to give me the chance.

When that chance finally came, I was happy to take it.

The next morning was perfect and dry. Unlike hunting in Iowa, I could see for miles in every direction. Was this the bucket-list kind of day that Karin and I had talked about weeks earlier?

We set up near a large field, and as day began to break, I could see a giant set of antlers moving in front of me. I turned to my cameraman and asked if we had enough light for me to shoot. He quickly answered no. So I had to watch as the big buck walked past at 60 yards in the dim morning light.

To my surprise, before too long, the cameraman felt like we had enough light to shoot. I quickly grabbed my rattling antlers and whacked them together before the Kansas giant walked out of sight. Even at 300 yards, the big buck heard the clashing. He immediately spun around and was now walking straight toward us. This buck had no idea we were in the area because the wind was blowing straight at our faces. Head down, he sniffed the ground as he walked within five yards. I drew my bow and took the shot. The arrow lodged firmly behind his shoulder. He ran less than 50 yards before I watched him go down.

As I approached, I could tell this deer was not the Boone and Crockett buck I had come to Kansas for. His rack, however, was by far the heaviest of any deer I had ever taken. In that moment, I realized that this buck was something I could check off my bucket list. Not because he was "the big one," but because of the new people I had met and the cool things I got to experience. Don't get me wrong—shooting a big deer is exciting. But having a hunting bucket list is about so much more than taking an animal. It's my prayer that *Raised Hunting* is doing a good job of communicating to hunters what we mean to each other and how important it is to approach hunting the right way. Like Easton says, "Have fun and live life."

That deer season, I learned a lot about having a bucket list.

First, we all need to make one.

Second, don't be surprised when the best things in your bucket aren't the things you expected.

Third, it's not really about what ends up in your bucket. It's more about the people, places, and things you get to experience along the way.

Have you thought about the bucket list of animals you've only dreamed of hunting? Take a few minutes to make your list.

_____

_____

_____

_____

_____

_____

——————— DAVID'S LIFE TIP ———————

Sometimes You Need a New Bucket

As a young boy growing up in Virginia, I often couldn't wait to go on my next hunt. Where we lived, the whitetail deer didn't have much size, and it was a big deal to kill a buck—any buck. I often prayed for even a spike to show up. I thought my deer-hunting opportunities would greatly improve after I moved to Arkansas, but I ended up being in the same boat. There were a lot of deer in Arkansas but not many big, mature bucks. At least not where I lived. Honestly, I never saw a Pope and Young type of deer the entire time we lived there. What I had envisioned and what I experienced were two very different things.

Maybe you can relate. As a hunter, you sit around the campfire the night before opening day of deer season and dream about what will happen the next morning. In your mind, you can see the perfect fall conditions for killing the buck of your dreams. You see yourself getting up early to a big breakfast of biscuits and gravy (that you can't eat because you're so excited) before climbing into your bow stand. You believe you'll only be sitting there a few minutes before you hear that familiar crunching of the leaves as Buckzilla makes his approach. You pick out the spot on your wall where you'll hang the mount after releasing the perfect arrow.

Does that sound familiar? I'm guessing it does, but that is usually not the way it happens. Instead of biscuits and gravy, you munch on a cherry Pop-Tart, and Buckzilla turns out to be the scrawniest little doe you've ever seen. One time I even arrived at my tree stand to discover that a beaver had cut down the tree it was hanging in!

Sometimes life is like that. What you thought was going to happen is nothing like what really happens. However, just as in hunting, that's not necessarily a bad thing. I love to hunt even when the conditions are not what I had been planning on. In life, the conditions will change as well, and the things you thought you really wanted to check off your bucket list often get pushed to the back burner. Life has a way of shifting your priorities. As I mentioned earlier, I've always wanted to hunt a brown bear in Alaska. However, if you told me I could either get on a plane tomorrow with a cameraman and go hunt a brown bear in Alaska or go turkey hunting in Iowa with my kid, I would choose the turkey hunt. When I say we envision the future, we sometimes don't envision the truth, and I think it's because we have no way of knowing what life will bring us. It's okay to experience a shift in your priorities. Your bucket list will change as you do. In my book, that's a good thing.

There's one more thing that is important about having a bucket list for your life. A bucket list isn't always about the big things that are almost unattainable—things like eating frog legs on top of Mount Kilimanjaro. Having a bucket list might mean going back to college, talking to your mom again after two years of silence, losing those extra pounds, or getting away for the weekend with your spouse.

Now would be a good time to pause and create a life bucket list.

Think about what's important to you at this moment. What's on your list?

_____

_____

_____

_____

_____

_____

DAVID'S FAITH TIP

Only God Can Fill Your Bucket

The closer I get to God, the more I feel like I'm in touch with what truly makes me happy. I still don't have all the answers, but I can tell you that when I was living with only David Holder in mind, no matter what I did, it was never enough. But having Jesus in my life makes everything I do more than enough. All the drinking and partying I did when I was younger only left me empty, but when I found Jesus, that emptiness was replaced with fullness. I'm happy and grateful to tell you that I'm no longer living for myself. I'm living for Him and for others. That doesn't mean that I've stopped chasing my dreams and goals. It does, however, mean that my priorities have shifted. It's taken me a while, but I'm finally at a place where I know that only Jesus can fill my bucket. Having a bucket list is one thing; having a full bucket is another.

I don't want to be so caught up in my own pursuits that I forget the one who makes my life worth living. I believe that God also has a bucket list. Only His list isn't for Him; it's for me. God has a list of all the things He has in mind for me to do. Things that I've never even thought of yet. Writing a book was never on my bucket list, and yet here I am, writing my second book. I am proof that when you put God first, you might be surprised by what ends up in your bucket!

You have let me experience the joys of life
and the exquisite pleasures of your own eternal presence.
PSALM 16:11 TLB

When your date nights include going to church, your bucket will overflow.

STUDY THE ANIMALS YOU HUNT
David's Best Tip

It's been said that 10 percent of the hunters kill 90 percent of the game. What that really means is that 10 percent of the hunters actually understand what the animals are doing, while the rest of the hunters are just winging it.

I would venture to guess that most deer hunters know the difference between a button buck and a Boone and Crockett buck. But I wonder how many of them know that a whitetail doe will often stomp her foot and blow at a buck that is trying to get frisky with her, just as she does when she spots you in your favorite tree stand. Even if you aren't planning on harvesting a particular animal, you can learn a lot about that species just by watching and paying close attention to what that animal is doing while you're hunting.

I've watched as a deer that I had no plan to shoot employed what I call the "head bob." This is when a deer acts like it's going to take a bite of grass, only to snap its head back up to see if it can catch you moving. A deer does this when trying to figure out something it doesn't understand. Perhaps it saw you moving or heard something it doesn't recognize. When a deer can't figure out what the problem is, it will often resort to trickery.

If you are new to hunting or your hunts haven't been all that successful, the greatest tip I can give you has nothing to do with gear or where to hunt. The best way to improve is to start paying attention to the mannerisms of the animals you hunt.

For example, notice whether a turkey's tail is straight up (because he is strutting his stuff for the ladies) or cocked sideways (because he is about to run off an intruding tom). Or watch a deer's tail. If a deer's tail is up and the deer is running, it is most likely on alert and scared. But if a doe's tail is straight out in a horizontal line, chances are, the next thing you're going to see is a buck following her. A calm deer will flick its tail back and forth as other deer approach as if to say, "I see you coming."

I could fill a book describing the mannerisms of the animals I've hunted over the past 40 years. I urge you to keep your eyes open and study the animals you hunt. You will gain a wealth of knowledge about what makes them nervous, how they interact with one another, and much more. Animals can't communicate through text messages or emails, and their vocabulary is less extensive than ours, so they use movement, sound, and smell to speak to their buddies. If you can learn what they are saying and replicate what they are doing, you will join the 10 percent of the hunters who are killing 90 percent of the game.

This is my best tip, and I believe it will help you more than all the others combined. God bless and good hunting.

ENCOURAGEMENT FROM KARIN

Abundance

> He said, "Throw your net on the right side of the boat and you will find some." When they did, they were unable to haul the net in because of the large number of fish.
> **JOHN 21:6**

On this day, Jesus's disciples had trouble catching fish. I've often found myself in similar situations while hunting. Sometimes, no matter how hard I try or what I do, nothing works in my favor. That's when I occasionally catch myself wanting to give up.

For several years, David and I lived in the tiny little town of Olney, Montana. Located in the northwest part of the state, Olney is an old sawmill town that once prospered due to the timber sales to Burlington Northern Railroad. However, in 2010, when my family relocated to the area, the sawmill had closed, and the town was nearly deserted except for the local post office. To say it was remote would be an understatement. Many of our neighbors lived off the grid, and we were surrounded by national forest as far as the eye could see.

This may sound like a little piece of heaven, but there were definitely some challenges. We quickly noticed that the abundant wildlife we expected to find in the area was nonexistent. We later learned that the lack of animals to hunt was due to the overpopulation of wolves, mountain lions, and grizzly bears. The predators were simply eating all the elk, whitetail, and mule deer. There was hardly anything at all left for us to hunt.

Day after day, David and the boys and I would hike, scout, and call for elk. But we had no luck. Not a single bull responded. Warren and Easton were boys at the time, and on more than one occasion, their excitement turned into disappointment as our family hunts left us empty-handed. No matter what we did or where we went, finding wildlife seemed to be impossible.

I'll be the first to admit that I was struggling to stay mentally and emotionally engaged in our hunting adventures. I was also dealing with guilt because I had prompted our move to northwest Montana to advance my career. And my career was thriving—but my spouse was suffering and so was our freezer. There was simply nothing there.

Have you ever felt like that in life? That no matter what you do or where you go, things never seem to come together or work out in your favor? Jesus's disciples must have felt that way on the night their nets continued to come up empty. They had fished and fished only to experience the letdown of having nothing to show for all their hard work.

While in Olney, I finally told myself I had to stop worrying about our lack of success. If God wanted us to have wildlife to hunt, He would point us in the right direction. If not, He would move us on—which He did. After I came to that realization, the pressure lifted. I learned to enjoy the beauty of the mountains even when I didn't see a single big-game animal.

Looking back, I can see how our lack of success while hunting in Olney opened up the door for us to move to Iowa—the land of the giant bucks! Now I regularly see whitetail deer from my front porch.

The deer in Iowa are plentiful and healthy, and they have incredibly massive racks. The story of the disciples' failed fishing trip tells me that if I believe in God's plan more than I believe in my current failure, I too can haul in more than my nets can hold.

REFLECTION

In what areas of life are you not catching anything? What will you do to fill your nets? What is Jesus saying to you in this moment?

HARVEST LOGS

Every moving thing that lives shall be food for you.
And as I gave you the green plants, I give you everything.

GENESIS 9:3 ESV

THE DAY

Date and Time: _____

Type of Weather: _____

THE LOCATION

State and County: _____

Stand, Blind, or Stalk: _____

THE ANIMAL

Species: _____

Male or Female: _____

Points/Weight/Score: _____

THE SHOT

Weapon: _____

Distance: _____

MEMORIES

Did anyone join you on this hunt? _____

Was there anything funny, sad, tormenting, or exciting that happened?

_____

Did you get lucky, or did the hunt go as planned? _____

What were you thankful for on this hunt? How did the good Lord bless it?

_____

_____

God was with the boy, and he grew up. He lived in the wilderness and became an expert with the bow.

GENESIS 21:20 ESV

THE DAY

Date and Time: _____

Type of Weather: _____

THE LOCATION

State and County: _____

Stand, Blind, or Stalk: _____

THE ANIMAL

Species: _____

Male or Female: _____

Points/Weight/Score: _____

THE SHOT

Weapon: _____

Distance: _____

MEMORIES

Did anyone join you on this hunt? _____

Was there anything funny, sad, tormenting, or exciting that happened?

_____

Did you get lucky, or did the hunt go as planned? _____

What were you thankful for on this hunt? How did the good Lord bless it?

_____

_____

He was a mighty hunter before the L<small>ORD</small>; *that is why it is said, "Like Nimrod, a mighty hunter before the* L<small>ORD</small>."*

GENESIS 10:9

THE DAY

Date and Time: _____

Type of Weather: _____

THE LOCATION

State and County: _____

Stand, Blind, or Stalk: _____

THE ANIMAL

Species: _____

Male or Female: _____

Points/Weight/Score: _____

THE SHOT

Weapon: _____

Distance: _____

MEMORIES

Did anyone join you on this hunt? _____

Was there anything funny, sad, tormenting, or exciting that happened?

_____

Did you get lucky, or did the hunt go as planned? _____

What were you thankful for on this hunt? How did the good Lord bless it?

_____

_____

Whoever is slothful will not roast his game,
but the diligent man will get precious wealth.

PROVERBS 12:27 ESV

THE DAY

Date and Time: _____

Type of Weather: _____

THE LOCATION

State and County: _____

Stand, Blind, or Stalk: _____

THE ANIMAL

Species: _____

Male or Female: _____

Points/Weight/Score: _____

THE SHOT

Weapon: _____

Distance: _____

MEMORIES

Did anyone join you on this hunt? _____

Was there anything funny, sad, tormenting, or exciting that happened?

_____

Did you get lucky, or did the hunt go as planned? _____

What were you thankful for on this hunt? How did the good Lord bless it?

_____

_____

David said to Saul, "Your servant has been keeping his father's sheep. When a lion or a bear came and carried off a sheep from the flock, I went after it, struck it and rescued the sheep from its mouth. When it turned on me, I seized it by its hair, struck it and killed it. Your servant has killed both the lion and the bear; this uncircumcised Philistine will be like one of them, because he has defied the armies of the living God."

1 SAMUEL 17:34-36

THE DAY

Date and Time: _____

Type of Weather: _____

THE LOCATION

State and County: _____

Stand, Blind, or Stalk: _____

THE ANIMAL

Species: _____

Male or Female: _____

Points/Weight/Score: _____

THE SHOT

Weapon: _____

Distance: _____

MEMORIES

Did anyone join you on this hunt? _____

Was there anything funny, sad, tormenting, or exciting that happened?

_____

Did you get lucky, or did the hunt go as planned? _____

What were you thankful for on this hunt? How did the good Lord bless it?

_____

_____

*She rises while it is yet night
and provides food for her household
and portions for her maidens.*

PROVERBS 31:15 ESV

THE DAY

Date and Time: _____

Type of Weather: _____

THE LOCATION

State and County: _____

Stand, Blind, or Stalk: _____

THE ANIMAL

Species: _____

Male or Female: _____

Points/Weight/Score: _____

THE SHOT

Weapon: _____

Distance: _____

MEMORIES

Did anyone join you on this hunt? _____

Was there anything funny, sad, tormenting, or exciting that happened?

_____

Did you get lucky, or did the hunt go as planned? _____

What were you thankful for on this hunt? How did the good Lord bless it?

_____

_____

For in him all things were created: things in heaven and on earth, visible and invisible, whether thrones or powers or rulers or authorities; all things have been created through him and for him. He is before all things, and in him all things hold together.

COLOSSIANS 1:16-17

THE DAY

Date and Time: _____

Type of Weather: _____

THE LOCATION

State and County: _____

Stand, Blind, or Stalk: _____

THE ANIMAL

Species: _____

Male or Female: _____

Points/Weight/Score: _____

THE SHOT

Weapon: _____

Distance: _____

MEMORIES

Did anyone join you on this hunt? _____

Was there anything funny, sad, tormenting, or exciting that happened?

_____

_____

Did you get lucky, or did the hunt go as planned? _____

What were you thankful for on this hunt? How did the good Lord bless it?

_____

_____

The heavens declare the glory of God;
the skies proclaim the work of his hands.

PSALM 19:1

THE DAY

Date and Time: _____

Type of Weather: _____

THE LOCATION

State and County: _____

Stand, Blind, or Stalk: _____

THE ANIMAL

Species: _____

Male or Female: _____

Points/Weight/Score: _____

THE SHOT

Weapon: _____

Distance: _____

MEMORIES

Did anyone join you on this hunt? _____

Was there anything funny, sad, tormenting, or exciting that happened?

_____

Did you get lucky, or did the hunt go as planned? _____

What were you thankful for on this hunt? How did the good Lord bless it?

_____

_____

Through him all things were made; without him nothing was made that has been made.

JOHN 1:3

THE DAY

Date and Time: _____

Type of Weather: _____

THE LOCATION

State and County: _____

Stand, Blind, or Stalk: _____

THE ANIMAL

Species: _____

Male or Female: _____

Points/Weight/Score: _____

THE SHOT

Weapon: _____

Distance: _____

MEMORIES

Did anyone join you on this hunt? _____

Was there anything funny, sad, tormenting, or exciting that happened?

_____

Did you get lucky, or did the hunt go as planned? _____

What were you thankful for on this hunt? How did the good Lord bless it?

_____

_____

God saw everything that he had made, and behold, it was very good. And there was evening and there was morning, the sixth day.

GENESIS 1:31 ESV

THE DAY

Date and Time: _____

Type of Weather: _____

THE LOCATION

State and County: _____

Stand, Blind, or Stalk: _____

THE ANIMAL

Species: _____

Male or Female: _____

Points/Weight/Score: _____

THE SHOT

Weapon: _____

Distance: _____

MEMORIES

Did anyone join you on this hunt? _____

Was there anything funny, sad, tormenting, or exciting that happened?

_____

Did you get lucky, or did the hunt go as planned? _____

What were you thankful for on this hunt? How did the good Lord bless it?

_____

_____

Praise the LORD, my soul.

LORD my God, you are very great;

you are clothed with splendor and majesty.

The LORD wraps himself in light as with a garment;

he stretches out the heavens like a tent

and lays the beams of his upper chambers on their waters.

He makes the clouds his chariot

and rides on the wings of the wind.

PSALM 104:1-3

THE DAY

Date and Time: _____

Type of Weather: _____

THE LOCATION

State and County: _____

Stand, Blind, or Stalk: _____

THE ANIMAL

Species: _____

Male or Female: _____

Points/Weight/Score: _____

THE SHOT

Weapon: _____

Distance: _____

MEMORIES

Did anyone join you on this hunt? _____

Was there anything funny, sad, tormenting, or exciting that happened?

_____

Did you get lucky, or did the hunt go as planned? _____

What were you thankful for on this hunt? How did the good Lord bless it?

_____

_____

He loves righteousness and justice;
the earth is full of the steadfast love of the LORD.

PSALM 33:5 ESV

THE DAY

Date and Time: _____

Type of Weather: _____

THE LOCATION

State and County: _____

Stand, Blind, or Stalk: _____

THE ANIMAL

Species: _____

Male or Female: _____

Points/Weight/Score: _____

THE SHOT

Weapon: _____

Distance: _____

MEMORIES

Did anyone join you on this hunt? _____

Was there anything funny, sad, tormenting, or exciting that happened?

_____

_____

Did you get lucky, or did the hunt go as planned? _____

What were you thankful for on this hunt? How did the good Lord bless it?

_____

_____

He has made everything beautiful in its time.

Also, he has put eternity into man's heart.

ECCLESIASTES 3:11 ESV

THE DAY

Date and Time: _____

Type of Weather: _____

THE LOCATION

State and County: _____

Stand, Blind, or Stalk: _____

THE ANIMAL

Species: _____

Male or Female: _____

Points/Weight/Score: _____

THE SHOT

Weapon: _____

Distance: _____

MEMORIES

Did anyone join you on this hunt? _____

Was there anything funny, sad, tormenting, or exciting that happened?

_____

Did you get lucky, or did the hunt go as planned? _____

What were you thankful for on this hunt? How did the good Lord bless it?

_____

_____

He makes me lie down in green pastures,
he leads me beside quiet waters,
he refreshes my soul.
He guides me along the right paths
for his name's sake.

PSALM 23:2-3

THE DAY

Date and Time: _____

Type of Weather: _____

THE LOCATION

State and County: _____

Stand, Blind, or Stalk: _____

THE ANIMAL

Species: _____

Male or Female: _____

Points/Weight/Score: _____

THE SHOT

Weapon: _____

Distance: _____

MEMORIES

Did anyone join you on this hunt? _____

Was there anything funny, sad, tormenting, or exciting that happened?

_____

Did you get lucky, or did the hunt go as planned? _____

What were you thankful for on this hunt? How did the good Lord bless it?

_____

_____

The earth is the LORD's, and everything in it,
the world, and all who live in it;
for he founded it on the seas
and established it on the waters.

PSALM 24:1-2

THE DAY

Date and Time: _____

Type of Weather: _____

THE LOCATION

State and County: _____

Stand, Blind, or Stalk: _____

THE ANIMAL

Species: _____

Male or Female: _____

Points/Weight/Score: _____

THE SHOT

Weapon: _____

Distance: _____

MEMORIES

Did anyone join you on this hunt? _____

Was there anything funny, sad, tormenting, or exciting that happened?

_____

Did you get lucky, or did the hunt go as planned? _____

What were you thankful for on this hunt? How did the good Lord bless it?

_____

_____

In the beginning, God created the heavens and the earth.

GENESIS 1:1 ESV

THE DAY

Date and Time: _____

Type of Weather: _____

THE LOCATION

State and County: _____

Stand, Blind, or Stalk: _____

THE ANIMAL

Species: _____

Male or Female: _____

Points/Weight/Score: _____

THE SHOT

Weapon: _____

Distance: _____

MEMORIES

Did anyone join you on this hunt? _____

Was there anything funny, sad, tormenting, or exciting that happened?

_____

Did you get lucky, or did the hunt go as planned? _____

What were you thankful for on this hunt? How did the good Lord bless it?

_____

_____

Worthy are you, our Lord and God,
to receive glory and honor and power,
for you created all things,
and by your will they existed and were created.

REVELATION 4:11 ESV

THE DAY

Date and Time: _____

Type of Weather: _____

THE LOCATION

State and County: _____

Stand, Blind, or Stalk: _____

THE ANIMAL

Species: _____

Male or Female: _____

Points/Weight/Score: _____

THE SHOT

Weapon: _____

Distance: _____

MEMORIES

Did anyone join you on this hunt? _____

Was there anything funny, sad, tormenting, or exciting that happened?

_____

Did you get lucky, or did the hunt go as planned? _____

What were you thankful for on this hunt? How did the good Lord bless it?

_____

_____

God so loved the world that he gave his one
and only Son, that whoever believes in him
shall not perish but have eternal life.

JOHN 3:16

THE DAY

Date and Time: _____

Type of Weather: _____

THE LOCATION

State and County: _____

Stand, Blind, or Stalk: _____

THE ANIMAL

Species: _____

Male or Female: _____

Points/Weight/Score: _____

THE SHOT

Weapon: _____

Distance: _____

MEMORIES

Did anyone join you on this hunt? _____

Was there anything funny, sad, tormenting, or exciting that happened?

_____

Did you get lucky, or did the hunt go as planned? _____

What were you thankful for on this hunt? How did the good Lord bless it?

_____

_____

Consider the lilies, how they grow: they neither toil nor spin, yet I tell you, even Solomon in all his glory was not arrayed like one of these.

LUKE 12:27 ESV

THE DAY

Date and Time: _____

Type of Weather: _____

THE LOCATION

State and County: _____

Stand, Blind, or Stalk: _____

THE ANIMAL

Species: _____

Male or Female: _____

Points/Weight/Score: _____

THE SHOT

Weapon: _____

Distance: _____

MEMORIES

Did anyone join you on this hunt? _____

Was there anything funny, sad, tormenting, or exciting that happened?

_____

Did you get lucky, or did the hunt go as planned? _____

What were you thankful for on this hunt? How did the good Lord bless it?

_____

_____

When I consider your heavens,

the work of your fingers,

the moon and the stars,

which you have set in place,

what is mankind that you are mindful of them,

human beings that you care for them?

PSALM 8:3-4

THE DAY

Date and Time: _____

Type of Weather: _____

THE LOCATION

State and County: _____

Stand, Blind, or Stalk: _____

THE ANIMAL

Species: _____

Male or Female: _____

Points/Weight/Score: _____

THE SHOT

Weapon: _____

Distance: _____

MEMORIES

Did anyone join you on this hunt? _____

Was there anything funny, sad, tormenting, or exciting that happened?

_____

Did you get lucky, or did the hunt go as planned? _____

What were you thankful for on this hunt? How did the good Lord bless it?

_____

_____

DAVID & KARIN HOLDER

with LARRY DUGGER

True Stories of *Faith, Family,* and
the *Adventure* of Hunting

SUCCEED ON THE HUNT
AND IN LIFE

◆————————▶

In bowhunting, being at full draw is the height of adventure, the moment when you're poised to take your best shot. Hunting enthusiasts and popular Outdoor Channel personalities David and Karin Holder believe you can live the same way you hunt—at full draw, excited and ready for whatever God has in store for you.

Each chapter is designed to help you take aim spiritually, physically, mentally, and on the hunt. You will go behind the scenes of David and Karin's television show, *Raised Hunting*, joining them in their thrilling outdoor journeys and learning how to prepare and cook healthy wild game with easy-to-follow recipes.

This book will help you become a better hunter. But more importantly, it will help you become a better parent, spouse, friend, and child of God, which is what living at full draw truly means. Discover that real fulfillment is a successful life, not a successful hunt. However, when you can find a way to bring those two things together, you've really got something to smile about.

To learn more about Harvest House books and
to read sample chapters, visit our website:

www.harvesthousepublishers.com

HARVEST HOUSE PUBLISHERS
EUGENE, OREGON